PIPPA MORGAN

CHINA'S COVID-19 VACCINE SUPPLIES TO THE GLOBAL SOUTH

Between Politics and Business

BRISTOL
UNIVERSITY
PRESS

First published in Great Britain in 2022 by

Bristol University Press
University of Bristol
1–9 Old Park Hill
Bristol
BS2 8BB
UK
t: +44 (0)117 374 6645
e: bup-info@bristol.ac.uk

Details of international sales and distribution partners are available at
bristoluniversitypress.co.uk

British Library Cataloguing in Publication Data
A catalogue record for this book is available from the British Library

ISBN 978-1-5292-2632-4 hardcover
ISBN 978-1-5292-2633-1 ePub
ISBN 978-1-5292-2634-8 ePdf

Cover design: Bristol University Press
Front cover image: iStock/Tijana Simic
Bristol University Press and Policy Press use environmentally
responsible print partners.
Printed in Great Britain by CPI Group (UK) Ltd, Croydon,
CR0 4YY

Contents

List of Figures and Tables

Figures

Tables

Notes on the Author

Dr Pippa Morgan is Lecturer in Political Science at Duke Kunshan University, Duke University's joint venture campus located in Kunshan, China. Her research focuses on the political economy of China's engagement with the Global South, including foreign aid, foreign direct investment, trade and contracting activity. Dr Morgan's academic work has been published in or is forthcoming in journals including *China Quarterly*, *International Studies Quarterly*, the *Journal of Globalization and Development*, *Oxford Development Studies* and *Third World Quarterly*.

Acknowledgements

Writing this short book would not have been possible without the support of a large number of people, to whom I am extremely grateful. First, I would like to thank the research assistants who helped to collect the quantitative data on China's vaccine supplies: Yuchen Ling, Chunyuan Sheng, Qunyi Zhao and Yiwei Zhao. Without their careful attention to detail and hard work, this research would not have been possible. Second, I thank the anonymous reviewers who provided extremely useful feedback on the proposal and draft. I am particularly indebted to the reviewer who provided detailed comments on the first draft of the manuscript, which greatly helped to clarify and strengthen it. Third, I am grateful to the many colleagues and friends who provided suggestions on my ideas and writing throughout the process. Fourth, I would like to thank Philippa Grand, formerly of Bristol University Press (BUP), for supporting my original proposal for this project, and her BUP colleagues Freya Trand and Rebecca Tomlinson for guiding it through the drafting and submission process. Needless to say, any errors are my own.

ONE

Introduction

On 13 January 2021, at Indonesia's Presidential Palace in the capital city of Jakarta, the country's President Joko Widodo received his first dose of the Chinese-made Sinovac vaccine against the SARS-CoV-2 virus. Media, including Chinese state news network CGTN, were invited to broadcast the event, which took place against the backdrop of a large red and white banner reading 'safe and halal vaccine' in Indonesian (CGTN, 2021c). Widodo was the first Indonesian to be vaccinated against the virus that causes COVID-19, closely followed by the country's health and military chiefs, in an effort to demonstrate the safety of the vaccine to fellow citizens.

At the time of Widodo's first dose, official data – which are widely understood to be a substantial underestimate – suggested that more than 24,000 Indonesians had already died of COVID-19 (Xinhua, 2021d). Over the following six months, Indonesia would become China's largest customer for COVID-19 vaccines, purchasing over 50 million doses up to the end of June 2021.

During the initial months of the global rollout of COVID-19 vaccines, China emerged as the key supplier to countries of the Global South.[1] Doses produced by Western manufacturers, on the other hand, were largely bought up by wealthy states in North America and Europe, which had seen severe health impacts from the pandemic, and made little effort to conceal their 'vaccine nationalism' despite warnings from the World Health Organization (WHO) of its pitfalls (Eaton, 2021).

China's status as the principal supplier of vaccines to the Global South sparked concerns among media, commentators and some policymakers that China was 'beating' the United States and other Western players in 'vaccine diplomacy' (Smith, 2021). Relatedly, suspicion arose that – as one article in the British broadsheet *The Times* put it – China aimed to use its vaccines to 'establish [a] new world order' (Tang, 2021).

On the other hand, Chinese officials worked hard to frame the country's vaccines as a 'global public good'. At a virtual event to launch the 73rd World Health Assembly in May 2020, as the first wave of the pandemic was subsiding in China but raging around most of the rest of the world, President Xi Jinping (2020) proclaimed: 'COVID-19 vaccine development and deployment in China, when available, will be made a global public good. This will be China's contribution to ensuring vaccine accessibility and affordability in developing countries.' Since then, the country's leaders, diplomats, and state media have repeatedly reiterated this framing, in an effort to bolster China's national brand and soft power (S.T. Lee, 2021).[2]

China deserves recognition for providing COVID-19 vaccines overseas during the initial months of the global vaccine rollout, when other manufacturing nations took steps to hoard them at home.[3] Moreover, in the context of the pandemic, the more companies that bring COVID-19 vaccines to market, and the more governments that give them away, the better for the world.

Nonetheless, the Chinese official framing as a 'global public good' is open to debate on both the 'public good' and 'global' dimensions, especially during the first six months of 2021 when early production capacity was limited and the gap between supply and demand was largest. During that period most (around 90 per cent)[4] of Chinese-made doses were sold commercially by manufacturers rather than donated by the Chinese government, and they were distributed unevenly, with some states receiving substantial numbers, and others very few or none at all.

Using empirical evidence, this book aims to go beyond both media narratives and China's official framing to contextualize, describe and explain the observable patterns in distribution of Chinese vaccine supplies. It focuses on the initial crisis months of the first half of 2021, when demand for vaccines vastly outstripped supply in almost every country around the world, and very few opportunities outside of China were available to the Global South. However, it also aims to draw broader lessons about Chinese vaccine supplies over the medium and long term.

In so doing, this book aims to highlight the importance of objective, empirical analysis of the economics and politics of China's overseas engagement. Explanations of Chinese behaviour – in particular those that influence government policy in North American and European capitals – tend to prioritize grand strategy and narrative over understanding the practical realities, and to deprioritize domestic and commercial imperatives within the country. In shedding light on the forces shaping the actual distribution in practice of Chinese vaccine supplies, this book hopes to contribute to more nuanced, empirically grounded discussion of China's role in the world, in tackling COVID-19 and beyond.

In brief, it argues that the patterns in the actual distribution of Chinese COVID-19 vaccine supplies during the first six months of 2021 were determined largely by the domestic economic and political context, as both the party-state and corporate actors engaged in 'opportunity management' (Jing, 2021; Kuhlmann et al, 2021), utilizing the window of the crisis to pursue their respective yet interrelated interests. More specifically, with a 'zero-COVID' strategy of pandemic control having become a critical aspect of the state's legitimacy at home, the Chinese government sought to utilize donations of vaccines to guard against so-called 'imported infections' coming to China from neighbouring states, while at the same time mitigating against risks of regional instability and bolstering established partnerships. The result was that during the period in question *donated* doses were largely concentrated in nearby Asian states and in particular those with pre-existing friendly relations with China (and not – as is often assumed – in Africa).

Meanwhile, Chinese commercial manufacturers, which pre-pandemic were relatively weak players in the global vaccine business, seized the opportunity to vastly expand their position in international markets. In this effort, they received state financial and administrative support, as central and local governments repackaged existing tools aiming to drive scientific innovation toward coronavirus vaccines. Consequently, China's overseas vaccine *sales*, which made up the vast majority of supplies, flowed mainly to populous middle-income states in Asia and Latin America (that is to say those with populations that needed them and, crucially, the money to buy them). Moreover, those states – including Joko Widodo's Indonesia – that had been willing and able to collaborate with Chinese vaccine manufacturers to host clinical trials (which had to take place overseas due to low case rates at home) were able to secure priority purchases. As with donations, Africa (with a few notable exceptions) was not prioritized.

This introductory chapter sets the scene for this analysis. It first describes the developmental and health impacts of the COVID-19 pandemic in the Global South, as well as the inequities in global vaccine supplies, in particular during the first wave of the vaccine rollout. During those initial months, vaccine nationalism in the West created a gap for alternative sources such as China to step in to. It then situates the book in context by reviewing existing understandings both of China's relationship with the Global South, and of the political economy of crises. Next, the chapter summarizes the analytical framework and main argument: namely that the distribution of Chinese COVID-19 vaccines was shaped by the 'opportunity management' of state and corporate actors, with the former seeking to consolidate their performance-based legitimacy and the latter to expand internationally into new products and markets. Finally, the chapter describes the data sources and provides a roadmap of the book.

COVID-19 and the Global South

COVID-19 both exposed and exacerbated existing inequalities between countries. As the economist and Nobel laureate Joseph Stiglitz (2020) points out, the virus 'goes disproportionately after the poor', both in health and economic terms. Moreover, the unequal health and economic impacts of the pandemic are interlinked. In particular, large parts of the Global South that have long been economically dependent on primary resource extraction were reliant on other states for manufactured products. This was brought into stark relief in the international scramble for manufactured medical goods such as masks, testing supplies, and later for vaccines.

Health impacts

By the end of 2020, two weeks before President Widodo received his first Sinovac shot, almost 84 million cases globally of COVID-19 had been reported to the WHO, alongside almost 2 million deaths (WHO, n.d.). These figures are an underestimate, as testing capacity was limited around the world (Wu et al, 2020; Irons and Raftery, 2021; Mwananyanda et al, 2021). Several low- and middle-income states were initially highly praised for their rapid and professionalized pandemic responses, informed by substantial on-the-ground experience in epidemiology and public health, and helped by having younger and less vulnerable populations (Anoko et al, 2020; Patterson and Balogun, 2021).

However, there are substantial difficulties associated with measurement of the health impact of the pandemic, in particular in low- and middle-income states with limited testing and statistical reporting. Without the ability to identify and test all cases of the disease, one option is to compare excess mortality rates, which use the gap between expected deaths (in a non-pandemic world) and actual deaths to evaluate COVID-19's impact. When estimated in this way, some analysts suggest that low- and middle-income states may have been in fact hit even harder in terms of deaths than their high-income counterparts in the initial waves (Gill and Schellekens, 2021). As discussed later in this chapter, vaccine inequities have widened this gap (Asundi et al, 2021).

Economic impacts

The economic impacts of the pandemic have also been substantial in the Global South, and exacerbated by existing inequalities. According to the World Bank (2021, p 30), in low-income countries the pandemic drove 2020 GDP growth to its lowest level in 27 years. In emerging market and developing economies more broadly, aggregate output dropped by 1.7 per cent in 2020.

Crucially, wealthier states were able to use both their economic resources and manufacturing capacity to secure supplies of critical commodities to assist in managing the health crisis. For example, while almost all countries faced shortages of masks, ventilators, and other supplies during the first wave (Burki, 2020), these shortages were worse in most states of the Global South (Jensen et al, 2021). While a small number of countries of the Global South are major PPE manufacturers, such as Indonesia, Malaysia, and Thailand (Park et al, 2020), the majority lacked the domestic capacity to manufacture their own supplies at scale, and the financial resources to source them in substantial quantities in the global marketplace.

Likewise, in the case of vaccines, as the next section details, in the initial months of mass vaccination rollout North America and Europe used their greater economic capacity to hold on to vaccine supplies from their own pharmaceutical firms and those of other manufacturers (Ibrahim, 2021). The result was that Global South states without domestic coronavirus vaccine development and manufacturing capabilities – which was almost all of them – either turned to China (and to some extent India) as an alternative, or were left without.

Why understanding Chinese vaccine supplies to the Global South matters

In late 2020 and early 2021, there was cautious optimism around the globe that the recent successes in vaccine development would offer a way out of the worst effects of the pandemic. In the UK, for example, the BBC asked 'Can we really jab our way out of lockdown?' (Triggle, 2021). UK citizens had good reason for this relative optimism, as did those in many other high-income states. The UK's mass vaccination programme had begun on 8 December 2020, when 91-year old Margaret Keenan became the first person to receive a COVID-19 vaccine dose outside of clinical trials. With a few bumps along the way, the UK did, in general, 'jab' itself out of lockdown. Mass vaccinations in the United States began the following week, and proceeded at pace, with a majority of US residents having received at least one shot by June 30 2021 (Our World in Data, n.d.). In nations with high vaccination coverage, vaccinations have successfully broken (to a significant extent) the link between catching COVID-19 and getting very ill and/or dying from it.

However, amid these welcome developments in the Global North, the WHO and the international scientific community pointed to emerging inequalities in vaccine distribution patterns and speeds. At the beginning of mass vaccinations in January 2021, WHO Director-General Dr Tedros Adhanom Ghebreyesus called on the world to 'work together as one global family to prioritize those most at risk' (WHO, 2021b). By June of that year, however, Dr Tedros was warning about a 'two track pandemic' as developed states continued to vaccinate healthy young adults while vulnerable people and healthcare workers went without in poorer nations (WHO, 2021a).

As Huang Yanzhong, a prominent US-based expert on China's role in global health, told the US news network CNBC in June 2021, for the first half-year of the global mass vaccine rollout China was 'almost the only primary player' in dispatching vaccines to the Global South (Y.N. Lee, 2021). Given China's strict pandemic control at home, cases and deaths within the country were extremely low compared to the rest of the world, which meant that China did not have to take extraordinary defensive steps such as vaccine export bans or huge advance pre-purchases to keep as many doses as possible at home. As such, the author's data (described in more detail later in this chapter) suggest that over 220 million doses of Chinese-made vaccines were delivered to Global South countries by mid-2021.

However, distribution of Chinese vaccines was also highly uneven, with some nations (mainly in Asia and Latin America) receiving extremely large numbers, and others (mainly in Africa) very few or none at all. Contextualizing, understanding and charting these patterns during the first six months of 2021, in which the gap between demand and supply was greatest and China was the near sole supplier to the Global South, is the primary focus of this book.

This broad geographic but limited temporal scope is deliberate: covering the 'first wave' of COVID-19 vaccine supplies to the Global South facilitates generalizable insights on state behaviour, aid and trade in times of crisis and highly constrained supply (as opposed to routine transactions). The end of June 2021 was chosen as a cut-off point because it is around this time that other major vaccine providers such as the US opened up and started allowing large scale shipments to the Global South (KFF, 2022), ending China's near monopoly; and because it is the point at which China considered its vaccine supplies to be sufficient to begin a policy of universal vaccination domestically (Mathieu et al, 2021). Nonetheless, the concluding chapter will consider a longer period and offer some tentative analysis on the future of Chinese vaccine supplies in the Global South.

There are several reasons why analysing and explaining these patterns is important. First, understanding the dynamics of Chinese overseas vaccine supplies has substantial practical relevance. Although countries in North America, Europe and elsewhere greatly increased their willingness to provide doses to the Global South[5] after completing initial domestic rollouts, China is likely to remain one of the world's major sources of COVID-19 vaccines going forward. As is elaborated in the concluding chapter, COVID-19 appears to be here to stay, and vaccination against it is likely to become a routine feature of life rather than a one-off event. Understanding the factors that determine Chinese vaccine supplies is therefore important to policymakers and other decision makers.[6]

Second, for those interested in China's foreign economic and political relations, the case of COVID-19 vaccine supplies offers an opportunity to generate generalizable insights on this topic. In the context of the Belt and Road Initiative (BRI) – President Xi Jinping's umbrella term for the country's goal of building economic and political connections along the historical Silk Road and beyond – China's relationship with (fellow) Global South countries is an increasingly important aspect of its foreign relations. Likewise, by delving into how the domestic economic and political context shaped vaccine development and distribution, this analysis also contains lessons for students of China's politics and economy.

Third, for scholars of international political economy (IPE), this topic presents an opportunity to analyse state behaviour, commercial interests and flows of a critical commodity in a time of crisis. Adapting on existing frameworks which see crises as a 'window of opportunity' for political actors (Jing, 2021; Kuhlmann et al, 2021), this book emphasizes the role of corporate actors and state–corporate linkages in 'opportunity management' during crises.

The following section gives a brief overview of existing scholarship on China and the Global South and the political economy of crises. (Readers who are more interested in the practical analysis should feel free to skip over this section.)

China, the Global South and crises

China and the Global South

Media narratives in North America and Western Europe typically portray China as pursuing a singular international political strategy decided at the top, with little role for domestic and/or corporate dynamics. For example, the BRI has been described by *Vox* as a 'trillion dollar plan' to 'become the world's next superpower' (Ellis, 2018), while Chinese vaccine supplies have been described by *Washington Post* columnist Josh Rogin (2021) as part of a grand strategy to 'pressure governments across the Western Hemisphere'. The idea that China is trying to use vaccines to control smaller, economically weaker countries and so create a new 'world order' (Tang, 2021) is an extreme manifestation of these narratives.

Viewed from this angle, both aid and trade are mere instruments of international statecraft for the central leadership. In line with this perspective, the (still small at the time of writing) academic literature on the IPE of COVID-19 vaccines in general conceptualizes them as a tool with which provider states can build soft power and promote their national brand (Cull, 2021; Hossain, 2021; S.T. Lee, 2021; Mol et al, 2021). More broadly, China's supplies of masks, other healthcare products, and medical personnel abroad have also been analysed as strategically deployed instruments of public diplomacy and soft power (Kobierecka and Marcin, 2021).

Chinese leaders and diplomats have clearly used rhetoric around the country's vaccine supplies to build Chinese soft power. In that sense, vaccines are a tool of statecraft. However, this book argues that patterns in the *actual distribution* of Chinese vaccine supplies to the Global South during the initial rollout were primarily driven by the interplay between domestic political and commercial interests.

Indeed, many scholars of Chinese politics have long asserted that China's behaviour is best understood as determined not by a top–down grand strategy but by a complex set of domestic interests that may or may not be in line with each other. In the academic literature, this is known as 'fragmented authoritarianism' (Lieberthal and Oksenberg, 1988; Lieberthal and Lampton, 1992; Shirk, 1993). Fragmented authoritarianism refers to the way in which the interests of, and bargaining between, different domestic actors shape Chinese policymaking and implementation.[7]

While some have questioned whether this model remains relevant given Xi Jinping's more centralized approach to governing, it remains the dominant framework for academic scholarship on Chinese policy processes (Brødsgaard, 2017), and a number of scholars have implicitly or explicitly applied this approach to understand the country's relations with the Global South (Breslin, 2013; Varrall, 2016; Zhang and Smith, 2017). This book shares the 'fragmented authoritarianism' literature's goal of understanding how different institutional interests determine China's behaviour. However, it departs from it in emphasizing the role of the state as a coordinated and coordinating actor in periods of crisis (Schwartz and Evans, 2007).

A related body of literature emphasizes the role of Chinese corporate actors, including both private firms and state owned enterprises (SOEs), in shaping the country's behaviour overseas. For example, Ye's (2020) analysis illustrates how the implementation of the BRI is shaped largely by the interests of subnational and commercial actors, which interpret the initiative as best suits their own commercial and/or political interests. William Norris (2016) analyses the contexts in which the Chinese state either succeeds or does not succeed in utilizing commercial actors to achieve political and strategic goals abroad. This book is informed by and contributes to literature that emphasizes the agency of commercial actors in Chinese economic engagement abroad (Liou, 2009,

2014; Norris, 2016; Morgan, 2019; Ye, 2020). However, as mentioned earlier, it emphasizes state–corporate linkages and the coordinating role of the government in sharing information across and strategically directing resources to firms during crises.

Political economy in times of crisis

While studies of crises are commonplace in the field of international security, the mainstream academic study of IPE has largely (although not exclusively) focused on the political causes and consequences of day-to-day exchanges of finance, goods, or other resources. In part this is because the dominant paradigm – Open Economy Politics (OEP) – rests on neoclassical economic assumptions, namely equilibria determined by demand and supply and rational, utility maximizing decision making units (Lake, 2009). Such assumptions do not sit easily with crises, which are characterized by 'threat, time pressure, and uncertainty' (Lipscy, 2020), and are likely to entail imperfect information, sudden changes in demand and supply, and fluctuating transactions costs.

However, the COVID-19 pandemic has naturally (re) illustrated the relevance of crises to scholars of IPE (Lipscy, 2020; Cotula, 2021). Some existing studies see crises as critical junctures in the reshaping of economics and politics, either negatively (Klein, 2008; Klein and Smith, 2008) or positively (Tsoukalis, 2012). Viewed from this perspective, crises – including pandemics – are catalysts of change, as actors seek either to capitalize on the situation in their own interests, or simply to cope with new threats and uncertainties.

Given that COVID-19 prompted dramatic changes in both ideas and policy across issue areas as diverse as global supply chains, the role of the state in the provision of social safety nets, and personal freedoms, it seems reasonable to view the pandemic in this light. One early exploratory analysis points to COVID-19 as a catalyst for disruption in governance (Cotula,

2021). In a critique of the political economy of the pandemic, Marshall and Correa (2020) point out that it has opened new space for commercial actors such as Zoom to take advantage of the situation.

On the other hand, some analyses point to the importance of historical continuity and existing structures in determining behaviour and outcomes during crises. For example, Henao-Kaffure and Hernandez-Álvarez's (2020) research into the 2009–10 Swine Flu pandemic contends that the global response was shaped by pre-existing commercial interests. Boettke and Powell (2021) argue that existing institutional political structures in the United States shaped economically suboptimal policy responses to the COVID-19 pandemic. A case study from the UK highlights how policymakers responded to that same crisis by turning to familiar outsourcing firms they had worked with in the past to source crucial items such as personal protective gear (Jones and Hameiri, 2021).

In practice, it seems clear that crises are both catalysts of change and conditioned by existing structures and patterns: these are two sides of the same coin. Proposing a framework to analyse differences across countries in response to the pandemic, Kuhlmann et al (2021) argue that actors seek opportunity from crisis, but the way in which they do so is shaped by existing institutional settings, government structures, and the pursuit of rational interests by actors within a given context. Jing Yijia (2021) applies this framework to analyse China's management of the pandemic domestically, arguing that existing institutions and structures allowed the Chinese government to bring the initial domestic outbreak under control comparatively quickly, with corresponding benefits for legitimacy and public trust in the ruling party.

As outlined in the next section, the framework and argument in this book draws on Kuhlmann et al (2021) and Jing's (2021) approach to understand how China's existing political and economic context shaped the distribution of its COVID-19 vaccine supplies to the Global South during the first half of

2021. However, it departs from Kuhlmann et al (2021) and Jing (2021) in focusing on outward facing – rather than inward facing – responses to the crisis. It also departs from these prior studies by analysing the role not only of political and administrative actors, but also of state–corporate linkages and the agency of corporate actors (which are – as the empirical evidence shows – principally responsible for the distribution of the majority of Chinese COVID-19 vaccines abroad).

Argument, data sources and roadmap

Framework and argument

Based on empirical evidence on where and how Chinese-made vaccine doses were delivered during the critical period of the first half of 2021, this book argues that they are best understood neither as a tool in a grand strategy of geopolitical competition with the West, nor as part of a scheme of altruistic free provision around the world. Instead, to explain the distribution of China's vaccine supplies to the Global South, we need to look *inside* the country. Borrowing from the concept of 'opportunity management' put forward by Kuhlmann et al (2021), this book argues that actors, including the Chinese party-state[8] and vaccine manufacturing firms, responded to the pandemic through 'usage' of the crisis in a manner that was shaped by the pre-existing political and economic conditions.

Essentially, China's 'opportunity management' during the initial vaccine rollout followed three steps. First, maintaining sealed borders and strict but localized pandemic control at home, to ensure cases and deaths remained as close to zero as possible, thereby contributing to the government's 'performance legitimacy' domestically (Jing, 2021). Second, targeting government donations of vaccines overseas to China's neighbourhood, with the dual goals of mitigating infections in border regions and maintaining regional stability, while at the same time bolstering established relationships. Finally, in the context of a long held (but as yet largely unfulfilled) aim of becoming a major global innovator in the pharmaceutical sector, which formed part of a wider drive to create a more innovation led economy, facilitate vaccine manufacturers to quickly develop and export COVID-19 vaccines to lucrative new markets.

To explain why China followed this strategy, this book's analytical framework proceeds in three stages. First, we need to understand the existing political, economic and institutional factors that conditioned the responses of key actors (the party-state and pharmaceutical firms). Next, from this basis, we can understand how and why these actors responded to the 'opportunity' of the crisis and subsequent question of overseas vaccine supplies. Finally, through understanding how and why key actors responded as they did, we can explain why and how Chinese COVID-19 vaccines were distributed around the Global South. These three steps are summarized in Figure 1.1, and explained in more detail in the following two sections.

Explaining China's vaccine donations

As laid out in Chapter Three, the central government is the key actor in the distribution of vaccine donations, which formed around 10 per cent of Chinese vaccine supplies overseas during the period in question.[9] Analysts of Chinese politics have long understood that China's ruling party relies on 'performance legitimacy' (Yang and Zhao, 2015). In other words, it derives domestic legitimacy from perceived effective governance, in particular of the economy but also in other fields. Likewise, maintaining stability in China's border regions is also an important aspect of performance legitimacy (Freeman, 2011). During 2020 and 2021, the party-state's strict control of the virus at home (after the initial loss of control in Wuhan in late 2019 and early 2020) also became a key source of performance legitimacy domestically (Jing, 2021).

One major consequence of pandemic-related performance legitimacy is substantial concern among leaders and officials

Figure 1.1: Explaining Chinese overseas vaccine supplies

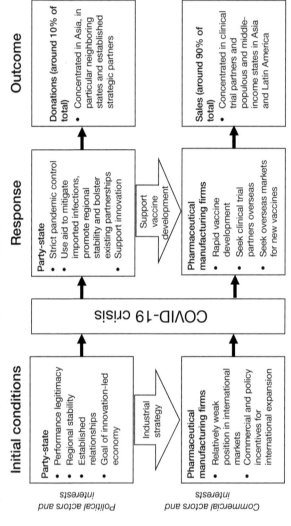

Source: Compiled by author, partially adapted from Jing (2021).

about 'imported infections' – cases of the virus entering the country through returning travellers or illegal border crossings. This is a significant challenge, given that China has a land border of over 22,000 kilometres shared with 14 other countries, each of which has had COVID-19 case rates substantially higher than China's. It is also highly interconnected economically and interpersonally, in particular with the Asian region (according to official statistics[10] over half of China's trade in 2019 was with other Asian economies). As a result, the Chinese government had a strong incentive to prioritize nearby states with a view to helping them manage the pandemic and thereby preventing imported infections in China, while also contributing to regional stability.

Nonetheless, China also has a long history of overseas health diplomacy and established international partnerships. COVID-19 vaccine donations largely followed established modalities of health aid, and were also used to consolidate existing partnerships, in particular in nearby states such as Pakistan in which a strong established partnership coincided with the goals of maintaining regional stability and mitigating imported infections. As a result (as illustrated in Figure 3.1 in Chapter Three), during the initial vaccine rollout in the first half of 2021, states which received substantial (rather than token) numbers of donated doses were largely concentrated in Asia, in particular those geographically close to China, and with already established strategic partnerships with Beijing. Africa, on the other hand, was not a priority.[11]

Explaining China's sales of vaccines

Different dynamics explained early sales of Chinese vaccines, which made up the vast majority (almost 90 per cent) of doses shipped to the Global South during the first half of 2021. Manufacturers of Chinese COVID-19 vaccines sold abroad during that period, which included the private firms Sinovac and CanSino, and the state owned Sinopharm, entered the pandemic with a relatively weak position in international markets, but strong commercial and policy incentives to expand their global reach, in particular in innovative products such as new vaccines. In the latter stages of clinical trials, they also faced an unusual challenge: low case rates in China meant it was difficult to test their products' efficacy at home, necessitating international partnerships.

Like corporations everywhere, Chinese firms have an incentive to sell their products overseas when they can profit from it. However, firms in the pharmaceutical sector, like other Chinese companies, have also been encouraged to seek markets abroad by successive waves of 'state mobilized globalization' (Ye, 2020). Starting with the Go Global policy in 2000, and more recently with the BRI initiated in 2013, the Chinese government has encouraged the country's firms to do business overseas, in part as a means of reducing overcapacity domestically. Relatedly, in the context of China's industrial strategy and Xi Jinping's emphasis on 'innovation driven development', which entails moving away from being the world's workshop for low-tech light manufactures and toward a global innovator, the state has also provided financial and other support for research and development (R&D) and corporate scientific innovation, including in the vaccine sector.

As is described in more detail in Chapter Four, in this context, Chinese vaccine manufacturers, supported by the government, used the 'opportunity' of the pandemic to quickly develop products in response to the new virus and thereby substantially increase their formerly weak international market share in vaccines. Sinovac, in particular, rose from relative obscurity to producing one of the world's most widely used vaccines against COVID-19. However, this process was complicated by the fact that Chinese vaccine companies had to quickly seek out overseas destinations to test the efficacy of their vaccines. Countries (such as Indonesia) that were able and willing to host clinical trials received priority access to purchases in exchange. As a result, early sales of Chinese vaccines were shaped both by conventional market forces (that is to say they were sold to large and comparatively wealthy emerging economies in Asia and Latin America), and by clinical trial partnerships between host states and manufacturers.

Data sources

The qualitative data used in this book come from publicly available information published by Chinese government departments, government press briefings, and press releases and other information from Chinese vaccine manufacturers, some of which is published in English but some of which is available only in Chinese. The analysis also draws on previous research (including the author's own).

Neither the Chinese government nor Chinese manufacturers have thus far released detailed, systematic information on their vaccine distribution. Therefore, the quantitative data come primarily from a dataset of Chinese vaccine supplies collected from publicly available sources by a research team led by the author. This dataset contains granular detail on Chinese vaccine supplies to countries of the Global South during the first six months of the global vaccine rollout. This includes information on dose numbers, commitment dates and delivery dates, as well as information on the type and nature of each batch of doses (including the manufacturer, whether supplies are commercially provided or donations, the type of organization supplying them, for example the central government, the People's Liberation Army, or – in most cases – via purchase agreements from the manufacturer), as well as a brief description in prose of each delivery or commitment.

The data were collected using systematic methodology that draws on publicly available Chinese language official sources, supplemented by reliable media sources.[12] In brief, this methodology involved four stages, beginning with highly authoritative official sources before moving to other sources to supplement official information:

- First, the research team combed the websites of three Chinese official sources: the website of the Chinese Embassy in the receiving country, the website of the Chinese Economic and Commercial Counsellor (ECC) Office in the receiving country, and the China International Development Cooperation Agency (CIDCA).[13] These three sources represent China's Ministry of Foreign Affairs, its Ministry of Commerce, and its foreign aid agency – the three main bureaucratic units involved in supplies of Chinese vaccines to foreign countries.

- Second, the research team combed Chinese official media sources, which, like the Embassies, ECC, and CIDCA, typically issue articles promoting commitments and deliveries of vaccines from China to partner states. These sources include Xinhua, China's official state press agency, *China Daily*, China's official newspaper aimed at foreign audiences, *People's Daily*, the Communist Party's flagship daily newspaper, and others.

- Third, the team combed (where available) relevant websites of recipient government official sources (for example the Ministry of Foreign Affairs, the Ministry of Health, and so on)[14] for press releases or other notifications of receipts of vaccinations from China.

- In the fourth and final step, the research team turned to other media/non-official sources via keyword searches using Google and the Chinese search engine Baidu to fill in gaps in information unavailable in official sources.[15]

Finally, the data underwent a quality control process in which entries with a limited number of supporting sources of information, as well as potential double counts, were checked and investigated by another member of the research team. The result is a detailed list of almost 400 instances of Chinese vaccine supplies to countries of the Global South during the first six months of 2021, which included more than 220 million delivered doses.[16] Figure 1.2 maps these

Figure 1.2: Map of delivered sales and donations of Chinese vaccines in the Global South, 1 January–30 June 2021 (number of doses)

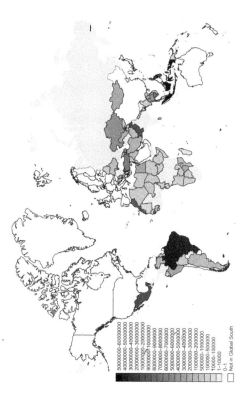

Notes: This figure includes both commercial sales and donations. Separate maps of donations and commercial sales can be found in Chapters Three and Four respectively.
Source: Compiled by author from own data, Copyright 1996–2022 StataCorp LLC.

Figure 1.3: Total delivered Chinese vaccines in the Global South, 1 January–30 June 2021 (number of doses, millions)

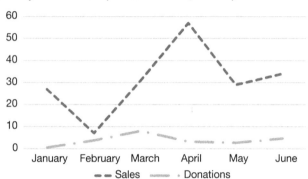

Notes: Donations include only official donations from the Chinese government or other state entities such as the People's Liberation Army. Does not include doses where the supply type (donation/sales) or delivery date is unclear.
Source: Compiled by author from own data.

doses, showing the concentration in Southeast Asia and Latin America. Figure 1.3 charts deliveries of donations and commercial sales over time, and illustrates that commercial sales vastly exceeded donations.

In addition to the quantitative data described above, this book also uses a number of other publicly available data sources on COVID-19 vaccines, and the pandemic more broadly. These include:

- Our World in Data's 'COVID-19 Vaccination Dataset', which tracks the global rollout of vaccines across multiple dimensions, including vaccinations administered per country and over time, donations to COVAX, and vaccine development (Mathieu et al, 2021).[17]
- The United Nations Children's Fund (UNICEF)'s 'COVID-19 Vaccine Market Dashboard', which provides summary data on bilateral and multilateral vaccine agreements, deliveries,[18] approvals, and prices (UNICEF, n.d.).

- Duke University's 'Launch and Scale Speedometer', which tracks vaccine purchases, donations and manufacturing deals around the world (Duke Global Health Innovation Center, n.d.).[19]
- The 'IMF-WHO COVID-19 Vaccine Supply Tracker', which aggregates data from each of the sources mentioned earlier in this list plus several others, to provide an overview of Secured and/or Expected Vaccine Supply per country (IMF and WHO, n.d.).[20]
- The consultancy Beijing Bridge's 'China COVID-19 Vaccine Tracker', which tracks and provides summary maps and charts of Chinese vaccines by recipient country (Beijing Bridge, n.d.).[21]

Readers should nonetheless bear in mind that each of these data sources, including the author's data, have advantages and disadvantages. For example, by using official Chinese sources as a base, the author's data risks undercounting in the rare cases in which China gives vaccines but does not wish to publicize it (as the unusual case of Myanmar illustrates in Chapter Three). On the other hand, several of the other aggregated sources listed above do not contain sufficiently granular information to analyse Chinese vaccine supplies in detail across geographical location and/or time, and may overlook valuable Chinese language sources.

More broadly, difficulties in ensuring access to reliable data about COVID-19 given cross country differences in reporting practices and statistical capacities are well documented (Farhadi and Lahooti, 2021), and only a small number of countries publish consistent detailed official statistics on their administered vaccines by source and/or manufacturer.[22] In short, no data – including those in this book – on Chinese or other vaccines is likely to be 100 per cent accurate all of the time. However, the author's data and all of the other data sources listed above are sufficiently reliable to make robust arguments about trends across space and time, and, wherever possible, the book makes use of multiple different data sources to support its claims.

Roadmap

The remainder of the book contains three substantive chapters and the conclusion. The next chapter lays out the pre-pandemic initial conditions that shaped China's 'opportunity management' via overseas vaccine supplies by contextualizing China's position in global health in recent history. First, it describes China's domestic health governance and its increasing importance to the party-state's performance-based legitimacy. Next, it charts China's role in bilateral health aid and international health governance institutions. Finally, it describes China's position in global pharmaceutical markets, which has expanded rapidly in recent years facilitated in part by the state, but nonetheless pre-pandemic was relatively weak compared to other major economies.

Chapter Three examines China's official donations of COVID-19 vaccines. It first briefly reviews competing narratives on Chinese vaccine supplies outside China ('grand strategy') and inside the country ('global public good'), and explains why neither is particularly helpful in explaining patterns in the actual distribution of donated vaccine doses during the first half of 2021. It then empirically charts those patterns, showing that – in line with the state's performance-based legitimacy goals – Asian neighbours were largely prioritized over traditional aid recipients in Africa. These patterns point to deliveries of donated doses being motivated by a pandemic-induced desire of Chinese officials to avoid 'imported infections' (and their potentially significant consequences for domestic legitimacy) and maintain stability in border regions, and relatedly by pre-existing strategic partnerships with the country's neighbours. Nonetheless, the way in which China implemented vaccine donations (bilaterally rather than multilaterally, and relying principally on SOEs for procurement) reflected its pre-existing approach to foreign aid.

Chapter Four focuses on commercial vaccine exports from Chinese manufacturers, which are the majority of Chinese vaccine doses administered abroad. It first reviews the histories of the companies involved, including Sinovac and CanSino, which are both relatively young private firms that were little known before the pandemic, and Sinopharm (officially known as China National Pharmaceutical Group Corporation), which is an established central SOE under the State Owned Assets Supervision and Administration Commission (SASAC). It then describes how these companies leveraged state support to quickly develop and bring to market their vaccine candidates. Finally, it maps patterns in Chinese vaccine sales during the initial mass vaccination rollout, which suggest they were driven by market forces and by clinical trial partnerships between manufacturers and host states.

The concluding chapter summarizes the book's core arguments and findings. It then discusses some broader implications of this analysis, both for China's foreign relations and for the international political economy of crises. Finally, the chapter concludes by looking ahead to the future of Chinese vaccine supplies overseas as production and exchange of COVID-19 vaccines becomes a routine transaction, noting both the challenges of increasing competition from other players and successive variants of the virus, as well as promising opportunities for further development, in particular in manufacturing collaborations in the Global South.

TWO

Contextualizing China's Position in Global Health

This chapter lays out the existing conditions that shaped the country's approach to overseas vaccine supplies during the pandemic. It first describes key aspects of China's domestic health governance and its increasing importance to the party-state's domestic legitimacy. It then chronicles the Chinese state's role in international health aid and governance, from traditional bilateral aid to a rising (but still somewhat limited) engagement in multilateral global health. Finally, it discusses Chinese companies' rapidly growing but still relatively weak pre-pandemic position in global pharmaceutical and healthcare markets, and their government's ambitions for them to become leading innovators in this strategically important sector.

Health governance in China

China is the world's most populous country, the world's second largest economy, and highly interconnected globally. It has also been a focal point in various disease outbreaks with international ramifications, including severe acute respiratory syndrome (SARS) in 2002–03 and avian influenza. China's domestic health governance therefore has important implications for global health more broadly. China's rapid economic growth and achievements in improving living standards of its population have greatly improved public health in the country (average life expectancy has increased by ten years since 1980, from 66 to

76 years[1]). However, the government has also faced criticism for prioritizing the economy at the expense of both health and, relatedly, the environment (Huang, 2020a), and for the vast inequalities within China's largely marketized healthcare system (Chan et al, 2009). A detailed overview of China's domestic health governance system, which is highly complex and has substantial subnational and urban–rural variation, is beyond the scope of this book.[2] The following paragraphs summarize the features that are most relevant to the main arguments of this book.

Performance legitimacy and infectious disease management

As laid out in the introductory chapter, China's party-state relies on performance legitimacy (Yang and Zhao, 2015). Since the initiation of reform and opening in 1978, when the ideological foundations of legitimacy under Mao was largely abandoned, (the perception of) effective governance has been central to domestic public acceptance of the Communist Party's right to rule China. During the first two and a half decades of the reform era, performance legitimacy was heavily centred on achieving rapid economic growth, with health, welfare and the environment deprioritized.

However, starting from the Hu-Wen era (2002–12),[3] the Chinese government started to rebalance, and emphasize social indicators including health and welfare alongside the economy. For example, new targets that focused on social welfare were introduced to local officials' performance evaluation criteria, a key mechanism for holding officials to account in China's non-competitive political system (Zuo, 2015).

Both public health and disaster management have therefore also become part of the party-state's performance-based legitimacy (Jing, 2021). Relatedly, triggered in part by the SARS crisis, China has paid increasing attention to institutions and processes for managing infectious diseases. The consequences of the SARS outbreak, which caused hundreds of deaths and severe financial and reputational damage, demonstrated both to citizens and to officials the economic and political threat posed by transmissible diseases, prompting securitization of the issue domestically (Chan et al, 2012, p 1). Essentially, avoiding and/or effectively managing major public health crises was now part of the bargain between the party-state and the population.

In response, China substantially increased its public health funding and established a new multi-tier disease control and prevention architecture. It also increased collaboration with foreign actors with greater technological capacity in disease surveillance, including in the United States (Bouey, 2020). These measures included the construction of the China Information System for Disease Control and Prevention, an internet based reporting system for real time case based reporting by hospitals and other institutions to local and national Centres for Disease Control (CDCs). These post-SARS updates to the Chinese disease surveillance system were commended by both Chinese and international scientists in journals such as *The Lancet* (Wang et al, 2008).

Nonetheless, China's domestic health governance is not always effective. Principal–agent problems exist at multiple levels of the system: central officials ('principals') are reliant on lower level officials and corporate and other non-state actors ('agents') to implement policies, and may lack the capacity and information to monitor them effectively. Likewise, officials in lower levels of the system face incentives to conceal unwelcome information for fear of punishment or damaging their promotion prospects. Indeed, recent years have seen outbursts of public anger, including protests, at health and safety scandals caused by local regulatory failures (Hernandez, 2018). However, the furious public reactions (and the corresponding harsh punishment of agents whose behaviour is discovered to have been at fault) highlight the centrality of health and disaster management to the party-state's legitimacy, and the risks that officials face to their careers and beyond when they fail to govern effectively in this area.

China's response to COVID-19 domestically brought these dynamics to light. Wuhan and Hubei officials reportedly concealed information about the severity of the initial crisis from the central government, illustrating that the principal–agent problem remains alive and well. However, once the crisis had been uncovered the state acted in a swift and coordinated manner (Deng and Peng, 2020). Consequently, the country's strict and relatively effective pandemic management from late January 2020 throughout the following two years, in particular when compared to most other major countries, became an important source of performance legitimacy. Survey data gathered by both international and Chinese researchers show that the pandemic response generally increased public trust in the government during the initial waves of the pandemic (Guang et al, 2021; Wu, Shi et al, 2021). Chinese residents – having enjoyed a negligible risk of falling ill, as well as a relatively normal life outside of short-term localized lockdowns throughout 2020 and 2021 – were broadly supportive of their government's 'zero-COVID' strategy, and in general expected their officials to manage the pandemic effectively.

As elaborated further in Chapter Three, these factors also shaped China's distribution of overseas vaccine donations, which served in part as an attempt to control the pandemic in border regions.

China in global health governance

China participates in global health through the provision of bilateral aid and engagement in multilateral health institutions, both of which have been the subject of controversy. With respect to bilateral aid, the country's motivations are hotly contested. The Chinese government's White Paper on foreign aid, published in April 2021, stated that China's aid is driven by 'internationalism and humanitarianism', and its responsibility as a major country (State Council of the People's Republic of China, 2021). On the other hand, some characterize Chinese foreign assistance as 'rogue aid', seeking to support dictators and exploit natural resources (Naím, 2007). Similarly, while some analysts point to major opportunities for Chinese engagement with multilateral health institutions (Joyce, 2018), others view China as exercising undue influence, in particular over the WHO (Feldwisch-Drentrup, 2020).

In practice, China's bilateral assistance is more established and extensive than its multilateral contribution through agencies such as the WHO. Beijing's health aid to foreign nations reflects a longstanding program of health diplomacy started in the 1960s under Mao Zedong. Its engagement with multilateral governance institutions, on the other hand, was comparatively limited prior to the pandemic relative to the country's size and economic might.

China's traditional health aid

China has been engaged in bilateral foreign aid for over half a century (Morgan and Zheng, 2019a). Its aid program was originally rooted in solidarity with fellow (then) socialist states, and with the more practical consideration of winning support for Beijing's claim to the Chinese seat in the United Nations (which was occupied by Taiwan until 1971) (Zhou, 2017; Morgan, 2018). China's traditional health aid mainly centres on three interrelated types of activity: Chinese medical teams (CMTs), donations of equipment and supplies, and construction of health infrastructure.

Beijing instigated the Chinese medical team programme in 1963 with the dispatch of the first team to Algeria (Li, 2011). The CMT programme involves the provision of small groups of Chinese doctors, nurses and support staff to a partner country, typically for a period of one to two years. After one team finishes their posting, they are replaced by another group of personnel from the same home province in China. In addition to treating local patients, CMTs also train local doctors, often in rural areas with very poor existing healthcare.

According to China's most recent 2021 White Paper on foreign aid, the most authoritative source of data on the topic, China has dispatched a total of 1,069 teams comprising a summed total of 27,484 medical workers to 72 countries and regions (State Council of the People's Republic of China, 2021). The core CMT programme has continued largely unchanged since the 1960s, to the extent that most of the same province–partner country pairings established under Mao Zedong continue today. Provincial actors' responsibilities for dispatching CMTs are the most visible representation of the long history that local actors have to play in China's health diplomacy.

However, more recently shorter-term specialized teams have been dispatched to address specific international health challenges. For example, in response to the Ebola outbreaks in West Africa in 2014, China dispatched disease control teams to Guinea, Liberia and Sierra Leone (Fan et al, 2015; Huang, 2017). Likewise, during the acute phase of the first wave of COVID-19 in early 2020, China dispatched short-term medical teams overseas to assist with dealing with the outbreak of the new disease.

China has also long provided bilateral donations of medical supplies and equipment to partner states, often alongside CMTs who utilize these goods in their work. For example, the expert teams dispatched to West Africa to fight Ebola in 2014 were accompanied by US$4.9 million worth of medical supplies, including personal protective clothing, disinfectants, thermometers, and medicine (Fan et al, 2015). Likewise, CMTs dispatched to tackle the first waves of COVID-19 abroad were also accompanied by donated medical supplies (Xinhua, 2020b).

Finally, China has also been active in building clinics, hospitals and other medical infrastructure, again since the

Mao era. These projects typically follow the 'turnkey' model, in which the Chinese government finances the construction, which is carried out by a state owned Chinese contracting firm, with the 'keys' handed over to the recipient state after completion. According to the most recent aid White Paper, China funded and completed the construction of 58 hospitals internationally between 2013 and 2018 following the turnkey model (State Council of the People's Republic of China, 2021).

CMTs are organized by provincial governments in conjunction with Chinese ECC offices in partner countries, and staffed by personnel from provincial hospitals. In aid projects that require a corporate contractor, such as turnkey infrastructure projects, funding is typically tied to the use of a Chinese contracting company (or set of companies) to provide construction and other goods and services. Historically, the market for Chinese aid contracts has been dominated by SOEs (Zhang and Smith, 2017). SOEs have closer ties to the state, and in many cases are descended from branches of the bureaucracy that implemented aid projects during the planned economy under Mao Zedong, and were later restructured into state owned firms (Morgan, 2018; Morgan and Zheng, 2019a, 2019b). However, some private firms, as well as former SOEs that have been privatized, are also active in the sector.

Pre-pandemic, China's health bilateral assistance was concentrated in Africa, which is the traditional locus of Chinese foreign aid across all sectors, and to a lesser extent in Asia. As China does not release systematic, detailed information on its foreign aid by sector and recipient, providing specific statistics on the regional distribution of health aid is a challenge. Table 2.1 utilizes data from AidData (Custer et al, 2021; Dreher et al, 2022), which aims to systematically track all Chinese development projects overseas from 2000–17 using information from publicly available sources, to summarize the regional distribution of Chinese health aid.

Table 2.1: Regional distribution of China's health aid, 2000–17

Region	Number of health Chinese ODA-like projects committed	Value of Chinese health ODA-like projects committed (US$)	% of total value
Africa	1,021	1,646,818,662	55%
Asia	157	831,644,139	28%
America	74	314,175,825	10%
Oceania	80	91,099,986	3%
Europe	25	62,885,662	2%
Middle East	18	49,819,994	2%

Note: Only includes projects marked as 'recommended for aggregates', belonging to the flow class 'ODA-like' and the sector 'health'.
Source: Compiled by author using data from AidData (Custer et al, 2021; Dreher et al, 2022).

China in global health governance institutions

While long a provider of bilateral aid, China is a much newer participant in multilateral health governance. Following the death of Mao Zedong in 1976 and the ascendancy of Deng Xiaoping to the paramount leadership in 1978, in the context of Deng's reform and opening to the outside world, China gradually became willing to participate in mainstream international institutions (Johnston, 2008), including the WHO (Liu et al, 2014).

Most notably, in 2006 China promoted the candidacy of Margaret Chan, a former Hong Kong public health official and Chinese national, for the position of WHO Director–General (Youde, 2018). Chan's candidacy was successful and she led the organization from 2006 to 2017. Prior to and during this period a series of crises, including HIV/AIDS, SARS and avian influenza, further deepened Chinese engagement with the WHO system, given both the practical necessity of cooperation on these issues and China's increased willingness to engage (Chan et al, 2009; Chan et al, 2012). More recently, China has sought to include the WHO in its BRI through the 'Health Silk Road' and, relatedly, the signing of Memoranda of Understandings on health security along the Silk Road (Tang et al, 2017).

However, Chinese financial contributions to multilateral health institutions have, even well into the reform era, remained substantially smaller than its bilateral investment in global health (Tuangratananon et al, 2019). While China's assessed contributions to the WHO budget (the percentage of GDP that each member country has to pay to the WHO) have been growing in line with its own economic growth, voluntary WHO contributions prior to the pandemic were relatively small.[4] Voluntary contributions form a major part of the organization's budget. As such, in 2018, China was only the 16th largest contributor to the WHO, trailing well behind the United States, the UK, the EU and Japan, as well as philanthropic organizations like the Gates Foundation (Moulds, 2020).

Moreover, China's emphasis on state sovereignty has limited its ability to engage with mainstream multilateral health governance institutions, including the WHO (Chan, 2011; Huang, 2018). In part as a result of experience of 'humiliation' at the hands of Western and Japanese imperial powers prior to the PRC's establishment in 1949, and the continued emphasis on this experience in China's patriotic education system, both the country's leadership and its citizens are highly sensitive to any perceived external 'interference' in China's internal affairs, including in public health. For example, during the SARS crisis China initially avoided sharing information with the WHO in part due to sovereignty concerns (Fang and Stone, 2012), and afterwards participated only in a limited fashion in the WHO's post-crisis revision of its International Health Regulations. As a result, China's participation in established multilateral governance institutions has been 'ambivalent' – professing a desire for participation and even leadership, but limited in practice (Youde, 2018).

Similarly, China's engagement in global health has been heavily state-centric, with a very limited role for non-governmental organizations (NGOs) and civil society more broadly. China's NGO sector is nascent and, while growing, the role of independent NGOs is dwarfed by that of 'government-organized' NGOs, known as GONGOs (Hsu et al, 2016). For example, the Chinese Red Cross Foundation (CRCF) has been active in providing international humanitarian aid, including health aid, in BRI regions (Lyu and Huo, 2020). The CRCF sits under the Red Cross Society of China (RCSC), which is in turn closely affiliated with and funded by the party-state (Hernández and Sui-Lee, 2020).

As is described in more detail in Chapter Three, these existing features of the China's approach to global health governance were to some extent reflected in its COVID-19 vaccine donations, which followed established aid modalities, including primarily sourcing from state owned firms and strongly favouring bilateral over multilateral cooperation. However, in line with the importance of domestic pandemic control and border stability in the party-state's performance legitimacy, initial overseas vaccine aid concentrated primarily on China's neighbouring region rather than on traditional partners in Africa.

China in world pharmaceutical markets

As Deng Xiaoping's increased willingness to participate in mainstream multilateral governance forums facilitated China's gradual engagement in multilateral global health institutions, his economic reforms simultaneously paved the way for the country's integration into the global economy. The pharmaceutical sector started to undergo liberalization from the mid-1980s (Yeung, 2002). As in other sectors, Chinese companies started out mostly with relatively simple and non-innovative products. However, in recent years – driven in part by the state's increased focus on innovation driven development – Chinese firms have sought to engage in higher tech fields, including development of new vaccines. Nonetheless, prior to the pandemic, their international success in this area was limited.

China's commercial pharmaceutical industry opens up

After the party-state abandoned Mao-era ideology as its basis for legitimacy in 1978, economic growth became the primary source of performance-based legitimacy. In turn, Chinese firms were encouraged, first in a limited way through Special Economic Zones (SEZs) in the coastal provinces of Guangdong and Fujian, and later at scale across the country, to produce goods for the global marketplace. China's initial comparative advantage lay in export of lower technology manufactured products. In the pharmaceutical sector, this included the active ingredients used by pharmaceutical firms in markets such as the US to make their drugs (Bate and Porter, 2009), as well as relatively low value added bulk generic drugs.

However, as a 'developmental state', the government retained an industrial strategy and strong guiding hand in the economy (Nee et al, 2007; Knight, 2014). At the same time as delivering growth through low cost manufacturing, the state also aimed to facilitate industrial upgrading and technological advancement. In the pharmaceutical sector, state funding was channelled into R&D from the 1980s (Wang et al, 2009), and the goal of becoming 'one of the world's pharmaceutical giants by the middle of the next century' was expressed as early as the late 1990s (Yeung, 2002, p 482). Various subsequent five-year plans and other policies identified the sector as a priority. However, hampered by lack of economies of scale, progress was initially slow and only 105 patents were filed in the United States by Chinese nationals in the pharmaceutical sector between 1978 and 1995 (Wang et al, 2009).

Around the turn of the century, two events accelerated the growth of China's position in world pharmaceutical markets.

First, China joined the World Trade Organization in 2001, which both boosted foreign trade and encouraged foreign investment in the pharmaceutical sector. Second, around the same time, the Chinese government promulgated the 'Go Global' initiative, a precursor to the BRI that aimed to encourage Chinese firms to do business abroad. Nonetheless, the majority of Chinese pharmaceutical firms, which were small and low tech, continued to face major challenges competing internationally given economies of scale in R&D, which advantaged large, established firms (Yeung, 2002).

The sector was also challenged by perceptions of low quality, even dangerous products (Bate and Porter, 2009). In markets of the Global South, China became a source of counterfeit medications (Morgan, 2019), and safety scandals both domestically and internationally undermined confidence in Chinese products. Figure 2.1 shows the value of Chinese pharmaceutical exports between 1992 and 2018, and shows that growth remained relatively slow until the mid-2000s.

Innovation driven development

In the Hu-Wen era and later under President Xi, who assumed the top leadership in late 2012, as China became richer and its industrial structure more advanced, the Chinese government's aim to move out of the cheap, low value added manufacturing model and create an innovation led economy intensified.

The 'Innovation Driven Development Strategy' was promulgated at the 18th National Congress of the Chinese Communist Party in 2012 (the same congress in which Xi Jinping replaced Hu Jintao as China's top leader). An outline published by the Communist Party Central Committee and State Council (Xinhua, 2016) explained that increasing China's role as a global science and technology hub was a key part of this strategy. Health was on the list of strategic priority sectors, with 'new types of vaccines' specifically listed as a goal. Likewise, the 12th Five Year Plan (2011–15) included a 'Key Drug

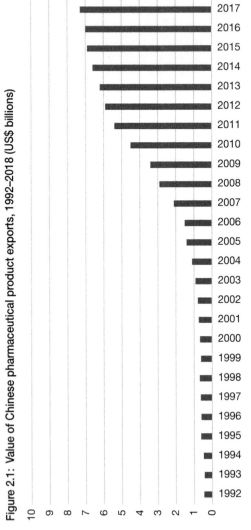

Figure 2.1: Value of Chinese pharmaceutical product exports, 1992–2018 (US$ billions)

Source: Compiled by author using data from UN Comtrade (n.d.).

Innovation Program', which earmarked over US$2 billion in funding for the sector across central and local governments. At the same time, private investment in pharmaceutical R&D also increased substantially (Qiu et al, 2014).

Much state support for Chinese R&D in the sector is channelled through the Ministry of Science and Technology (MOST), the lead bureaucratic unit with responsibility for driving forward scientific and technological innovation in China. At the same time, local governments have also sought to promote pharmaceutical innovation through the creation of special economic zones and industrial parks (WHO, 2017). These zones are designed to facilitate investment, as well as to bring companies in related sectors together to encourage collaboration, clustering, and technology spillovers. Meanwhile the 'Thousand Talents' programme, which provides lucrative rewards for Chinese scholars and researchers with degrees and/ or experience abroad who return home, aimed to draw leading Chinese scientists back to the country. The 'Made in China 2025' programme, which has attracted considerable suspicion from some Western governments, in particular the US, likewise aims to turn China into a centre for high tech production.

Nonetheless, despite efforts toward both sectoral growth and innovation, as an article by Ni et al (2017) put it, 'the intense Research and Development input has not brought about the expectable output'. While China's scholars and universities have become prolific publishers of new scientific literature in both English and Chinese, in terms of innovative commercialized products, at the start of the pandemic Chinese pharmaceutical companies remained in a relatively weak position vis-à-vis their competitors, especially those in Europe and North America.

Figure 2.2 shows China's total exports of pharmaceutical products compared to other major economies in 2018. As the figure illustrates, it remained relatively small compared to the United States, the European Union and India. The EU and US are home to major pharmaceutical firms that were household names long before the pandemic, such as AstraZeneca, Janssen

Figure 2.2: Value of Chinese pharmaceutical exports in 2018 compared to other major economies (US$ billions)

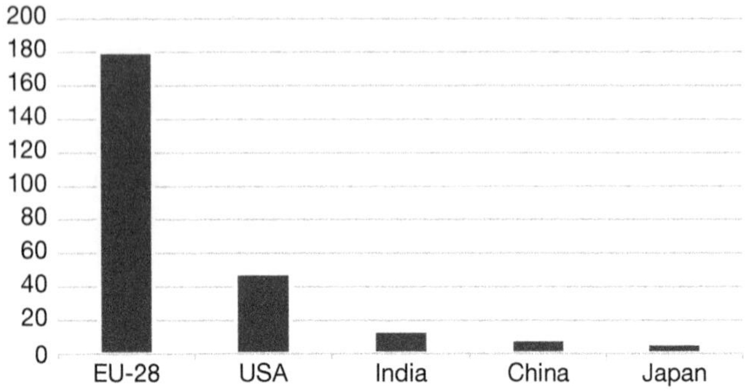

Note: Japan data are from 2019.
Source: Compiled by author using data from UN Comtrade (n.d.).

and Pfizer. India is another major manufacturer of active ingredients and generic drugs, as well as the home of the Serum Institute of India (SII), the world's largest (non-COVID-19) vaccine manufacturing firm.

China in global vaccine markets

China's pre-pandemic position in global vaccine markets reflects these broader trends: it has grown significantly since reform and opening, and in particular over the past decade, but nonetheless remained relatively weak compared to other major economies in the West, as well as India.

While Chinese firms have long manufactured vaccines for the domestic market, both regulators and companies were slow to demonstrate international standards. China's then-domestic vaccine approval agency, the China Food and Drug Administration (now known as the National Medical Products Administration, NMPA), did not receive WHO approval of its standards for vaccine regulatory oversight until March 2011 (Zha, 2021). Likewise, the first WHO prequalification[5] of a Chinese-made vaccine (for Japanese Encephalitis) did not occur until 2013. The prequalification was facilitated by collaboration with PATH, a non-profit in the United States funded by the Bill and Melinda Gates Foundation. At the time, a representative of the Gavi Vaccine Alliance Secretariat in Geneva called it 'a big step forward' and noted that 'now several other Chinese producers are interested in obtaining prequalification for their vaccines' (Parry, 2014).

As such, Shi et al (2017) argue that China has moved from being a 'vaccine production country' to a 'powerful vaccine-innovation country'. However, prior to the pandemic this was somewhat of an overstatement. As illustrated in Figure 2.3, Chinese vaccine exports have indeed grown from negligible levels in the 1990s to US$120 million in 2018. However, as shown in Figure 2.4, these remained substantially smaller than those of other major economies. Indeed, there were no Chinese-made vaccines among the top 15 in global revenue in 2018 (Hu and Chen, 2021).

As is elaborated further in Chapter Four, Chinese COVID-19 vaccine development and production during the pandemic reflected these pre-existing dynamics in that the state played an important role in providing financial and administrative support to the manufacturing firms in vaccine development (Hu and Chen, 2021). However, it also represented a break with the past, as Chinese corporate and state actors were able to utilize the opportunity of the pandemic to drive forward the share of Chinese companies in the world's vaccine markets, and in turn boost the country's position as a creator of new pharmaceutical products.

Conclusion

This chapter has laid out the pre-existing conditions that shaped the 'opportunity management' behaviour of Chinese corporate and state actors during the development and overseas distribution of vaccines in response to COVID-19.

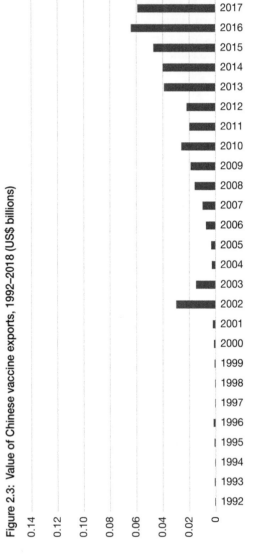

Figure 2.3: Value of Chinese vaccine exports, 1992–2018 (US$ billions)

Source: Compiled by author using data from UN Comtrade (n.d.).

Figure 2.4: Value of Chinese vaccine exports in 2018 compared to other major economies (US$ billions)

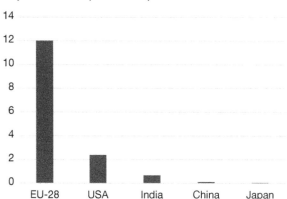

Note: Japan data are from 2019.
Source: Compiled by author using data from UN Comtrade (n.d.).

Domestically, the Chinese party-state is heavily reliant on performance legitimacy, that is to say (perceived) effective governance, including in public health and disaster management. Internationally, China's approach to global health has historically been focused on state-centric bilateral aid, with limited, albeit growing, engagement in multilateral governance institutions. As described in detail in the following chapter, these contextual factors shaped Chinese vaccine *donations* during the initial global rollout: substantive donations were concentrated in neighbouring states in an effort to safeguard regional stability and mitigate the risk of the virus travelling back into China, and followed established modalities of bilateral aid.

On the other hand, Chinese pharmaceutical firms faced the pandemic following several decades of growth and supported by strong links with the state, which increasingly aimed to support an innovation led economy, including the development of new vaccines. Nonetheless, they remained in a relatively weak position vis–à–vis international competitors. As is laid out in Chapter Four, in the context of both strong motivation to boost their market share abroad and financial and administrative support from the state, Chinese vaccine manufacturers were able to seize the opportunity of the pandemic to become some of the world's largest commercial suppliers of a critical new commodity: COVID-19 vaccines.

THREE

'Vaccine Diplomacy'

This chapter describes and explains China's official donations of COVID-19 vaccines to countries of the Global South during the first six months of 2021. The first section contrasts media narratives and China's official framing of its vaccine donations, before arguing that these rhetorical debates are not very productive in understanding the actual distribution of Chinese vaccine donations. The second section maps these donations empirically and analyses the factors shaping the choices of the Chinese government about where to deliver vaccines during the initial overseas rollout, including 'moving the anti-pandemic barrier forward' by mitigating the risk of imported infections, promoting regional stability, and strengthening established ties with neighbours. This section also highlights some similarities between Chinese vaccine donations and its established aid practices. The third and final section illustrates these dynamics through the case studies of Myanmar and Pakistan.

Narratives on Chinese vaccine supplies

China's economic engagement with the Global South has long been viewed with suspicion. In particular, the so-called 'debt trap diplomacy' narrative posits that China lures countries into debt in order to take control of their strategic assets (Chellaney, 2017). This narrative has been widely debunked by academic analyses (Brautigam, 2020; Singh, 2021), but remains influential among policymakers in North America and Europe.

China has similarly been accused of using vaccine donations as a tool of geopolitics. In February 2021, the *New York Times* described coronavirus vaccines as 'a new currency for international diplomacy' (Mashal and Yee, 2021), and the notion that a strategic programme of 'vaccine diplomacy' in competition with the West has driven Chinese vaccine distribution is pervasive. At its most extreme end this viewpoint situates vaccines at the centre of a competition for a 'new world order' between China on the one hand and the US and its allies on the other (Greenwald and Margolis, 2020; Tang, 2021). For example, in April 2021 an article in the prestigious *Foreign Policy* magazine argued that 'vaccines will shape the new geopolitical order', and contended that 'Russia and China have begun supplying vaccines in exchange for favourable foreign-policy concessions' (Frankel Pratt and Levin, 2021).

China, on the other hand, has consistently framed its vaccines as a 'global public good'. In May 2020, at the 73rd World Health Assembly, the Chinese leadership stated that the country's COVID-19 vaccines, 'when available' would become a 'global public good' (Pan, 2020). Since then, Chinese officials and state media have frequently reiterated this claim. The official framing emphasizes that China has delivered on its promises by actually having shipped vaccine doses to low- and middle-income countries during the early months of the global vaccine rollout, in contrast to Western states, some of which promised vaccines but all of which did not actually deliver them when most needed. As an article published by the main state news agency Xinhua (2021c) put it, official narratives stressed that 'China *walks the talk* [emphasis added] in making COVID-19 vaccines global public goods'.

It seems clear from Beijing's official pronouncements on the topic that it does aim to shape the narrative on vaccine supplies in a way that boosts its international image (S. T. Lee, 2021), as do other vaccine supplying nations such as the United States[1] and Russia. (Indeed, the latter's Sputnik V vaccine even has its own YouTube channel, Facebook page, and official Twitter accounts (Croft, 2021)). However, the fact that countries seek to frame narratives on their aid and trade in ways that improve their national image is nothing new.

In trying to understand where Chinese vaccine donations actually went during the initial months of their global rollout, the 'vaccine diplomacy' vs. 'global public good' debate is unfruitful. Neither side is particularly helpful in generating explanations for the Chinese government's decisions about where to prioritize its donations of vaccines. On the one hand, as the analysis below shows, the empirical distribution of Chinese vaccine doses does not point to an attempt to 'remake world order'. Doses were concentrated in countries in China's neighbourhood with good pre-existing relations with China, most of which were unlikely focal points of Sino-Western competition. On the other hand, in the context of the large gap between supply and demand, it was impossible for Chinese (or any other) vaccines to be liberally distributed overseas as a 'public good', as officials faced trade-offs between potential partner states, and between domestic and international needs.

Indeed, while Chinese manufacturers' production capacity has ramped up rapidly, in the initial months of the vaccine rollout it did not meet demand. Gao Fu, then-head of China's central CDC, stated in early March 2021 that he expected that capacity was sufficient to vaccinate just 40 per cent of the domestic population by the end of June 2021 (Reuters, 2021a). The following month, Chinese media reported on tight vaccine supplies in some parts of the country (McCarthy, 2021). China's comparatively very low case rates meant it did not face the same immediate pressure as most other countries to vaccinate at home. However, given very low exposure to the virus at home, without vaccinations China's population was even more vulnerable to COVID-19 than the populations of countries that had already undergone large scale outbreaks. Given the efforts of China's leadership to frame China's strict virus control as representative of the superiority of China's political system vis-à-vis liberal democracy, this 'immunity gap' between China and Western countries posed a potential problem for Chinese leaders if it undermined confidence in China's political system and approach to managing the pandemic (Huang, 2020b).

Chinese officials therefore faced a trade-off, raising the question of in what context they considered it preferable to give constrained supplies of vaccines away to other states rather than procure them for the domestic population. As the following section outlines, the empirical evidence on vaccine donations suggests that forces in favour of overseas donations included the goals of mitigating risks of imported infections and ensuring regional stability, while at the same time taking the opportunity to buttress established relationships.

Explaining the distribution of Chinese vaccine donations

Figure 3.1 maps deliveries of Chinese COVID-19 vaccine donations during the first six months of 2021. As the map shows, Chinese donations during that period were heavily concentrated in nearby countries.

'Moving the anti-pandemic barrier forward'

China is unusual in this neighbourhood focus,[2] which is rooted in the domestic political context. China's internal rollout of vaccines, which also was very different from other major countries, holds a clue to explaining these patterns. Unlike most nations, which first vaccinated the elderly who were most at risk if they were to become infected, China's primary aim, in the context of the 'zero-COVID' strategy, was to avoid the disease getting near to the elderly (or anyone else) in the first place. As such, it prioritized its residents living in border regions and groups such as airport workers and those involved in cold chain imports (Zhang et al, 2021). China's southwestern Yunnan province, for example, first vaccinated every resident of villages along its border with Myanmar, before moving inland.

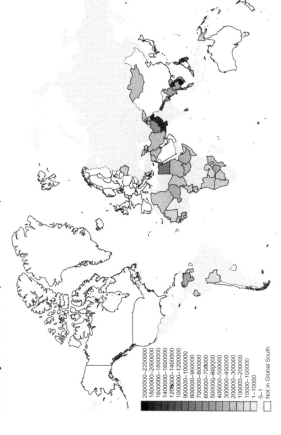

Figure 3.1: Map of delivered donations of Chinese vaccines in the Global South, 1 January–30 June 2021 (number of doses)

Maps compiled using Stata. Copyright 1996–2022 StataCorp LLC.

This strategy reflects the fact that, as described in previous chapters, the Chinese government relies on performance legitimacy instead of the electorally derived legitimacy of governments in competitive political systems, and strict control of COVID-19 has become an important aspect of that legitimacy. While Chinese residents contended with sealed borders and sporadic local level lockdowns during much of 2020 and 2021, they also enjoyed negligible risks of catching the virus, and a relatively normal daily life compared with those in many other countries. As a result, surveys carried out by a team from the University of California San Diego and Stanford University strongly suggest a high level of citizen confidence in the Chinese government at both central and local levels (Guang et al, 2021). During 2020 and 2021, the Chinese government effectively seized the opportunity of the pandemic to shore up legitimacy at home by controlling the virus more effectively than most other major states (Jing, 2021).

However, the corollary of this is that officials that are seen to have failed in successfully controlling the pandemic may be removed from their jobs and suffer serious career consequences (as happened to Hubei province and Wuhan city officials when the new virus first created a crisis in Wuhan).[3] More broadly, as Huang Yanzhong (2020a) argues, failure to address health crises presents a serious challenge for the party-state's performance-based legitimacy. Indeed, the consequences of failures in pandemic control have led to public critique of the government on Chinese social media (Feng, 2021; BBC News, 2022).

Accordingly, in the words of CIDCA's head Luo Zhaohui, vaccine donations were in part a means of 'moving the anti-pandemic barrier forward' (State Council Information Office, 2021b). Strong people-to-people and transport linkages with neighbouring regions and lengthy borders mean that pandemic control in South and Southeast Asia has important implications for China's domestic efforts. China's land borders have been officially sealed as a result of the pandemic, and the country has constructed extensive physical barriers along its southern border in an effort to keep COVID-19 out (Qi et al, 2022). However, nearly 50,000 people were arrested in 2021 for illegal border crossing or people trafficking in southwest China, which borders Laos, Myanmar and Vietnam (Wu, 2022). While empirical studies of the origins of imported COVID-19 cases by air travel (the main legal route into the country) are limited, one investigation into the southern Chinese metropolis of Guangzhou in 2020 found that Asia was by far the largest source of imported infections[4] by air (over 40 per cent) (Africa, by contrast, was the source of only 13 per cent, and Latin America 1.5 per cent, with the remainder from Europe, North America, and Oceania) (Zhang et al, 2020).

Similarly, the protection of Chinese citizens overseas has also become an increasingly important aspect of the party-state's legitimacy, particularly in the context of China's growing economic and human presence abroad (Zerba, 2014; Ghiselli, 2021). Accordingly, in March 2021 the Chinese government initiated the 'Spring Sprout' programme, which dispatches vaccines specifically for inoculating Chinese nationals living and working abroad. The programme was announced by Foreign Minister Wang Yi during the 2021 'two sessions' (the annual meetings of the National People's Congress and the National Committee of the Chinese People's Political Consultative Conference). As of early July 2021, over 1.7 million Chinese citizens in more than 160 overseas countries and regions had received vaccines through the Spring Sprout programme (Shen and Chu, 2021).

Maintaining regional stability and supporting established partners

Beijing has substantial material interests in regional stability, which is critical to China's economic growth and therefore to the Party's legitimacy and domestic security (Taylor and Cheng, 2022). Relatedly, maintaining stable border regions has long been an important aspect of that legitimacy. Researchers have documented a link between epidemics and social stability (Censolo and Morelli, 2020), and COVID-19 fuelled unrest in multiple states in Southeast Asia (Robinson et al, 2020). As such, in addition to mitigating the risks of imported infections, supporting pandemic control in neighbouring countries may also help to promote greater regional stability. Indeed, when asked to detail the specific achievements of China's overseas vaccine aid, CIDCA's head Luo Zhaohui further noted that 'it is difficult for China to remain peaceful and secure unless its neighbors are secure' (State Council Information Office, 2021b). Moreover, Li and Ye (2019)'s empirical analysis of China's global diplomatic partnerships finds that Beijing is more inclined to establish formal partnerships with neighbours, which they argue is an effort to create a more stable and secure regional environment.

China has three broad levels of formal diplomatic partnership with foreign states. At the top are 'comprehensive strategic partnerships', followed by 'strategic partnerships' and 'regular partnerships'. As Table 3.1 shows, of the top recipients of Chinese vaccine donations,[5] the vast majority had a pre-existing comprehensive strategic partnership with China, while the remainder had a strategic partnership. All had signed a Memorandum of Understanding (MoU) with China on participation in the BRI.

Both the above empirical evidence and public statements from Chinese officials suggest that the country saw vaccine donations as a means of simultaneously contributing to pandemic control while also seizing the opportunity to consolidate established relationships. For example, in describing the achievements of Chinese vaccine donations to Myanmar, Luo Zhaohui further noted that in addition to 'stemming a domestic resurgence', there were 'benefits that extend into anti-epidemic, diplomatic and political areas' (State Council Information Office, 2021b).

As well as having strong established relations with China, several of these countries provided the highest level of support for Beijing in early 2020 when the outbreak in China was at its

Table 3.1: Top recipients of Chinese vaccine donations, 1 January–30 June 2021

Country	% of total donations	Region	On China's border	Level of diplomatic partnership	BRI MoU signed
Cambodia	10%	Asia	No	Comprehensive strategic partnership	Yes
Pakistan	9%	Asia	Yes	Comprehensive strategic partnership	Yes
Laos	8%	Asia	Yes	Comprehensive strategic partnership	Yes
Nepal	8%	Asia	Yes	Strategic partnership	Yes
Sri Lanka	5%	Asia	No	Strategic partnership	Yes
Philippines	4%	Asia	No	Comprehensive strategic partnership	Yes
Egypt	4%	Africa	No	Comprehensive strategic partnership	Yes
Afghanistan	3%	Asia	Yes	Strategic partnership	Yes
Myanmar	2%	Asia	Yes	Comprehensive strategic partnership	Yes

(continued)

Table 3.1: Top recipients of Chinese vaccine donations, 1 January–30 June 2021 (continued)

Country	% of total donations	Region	On China's border	Level of diplomatic partnership	BRI MoU signed
Vietnam	2%	Asia	Yes	Comprehensive strategic partnership	Yes
Thailand	2%	Asia	No	Comprehensive strategic partnership	Yes
Bangladesh	2%	Asia	No	Strategic partnership	Yes
Zimbabwe	2%	Africa	No	Comprehensive strategic partnership	Yes
Venezuela	2%	Latin America	No	Comprehensive strategic partnership	Yes

Note: Donation data are from author's own data and include only donations that were delivered over this period (not informal or formal commitments).

Source: Compiled by author. Categorizations of partnership levels are from Li and Ye (2019),[13] and data on BRI MoU signature are from Nedopil (2021).

peak, including visits by national leaders to signal confidence in Beijing during the initial outbreak in Wuhan, a time of great uncertainty and fear. Cambodia's Prime Minister Hun Sen visited China in February 2020, while Pakistan's President Arif Ali Alvi made a visit the following month. These expressions of solidarity reflected the strong pre-existing ties between China and these countries.

Chinese vaccine donations to Egypt, its top non-Asian recipient over the period in question, likewise reflect a longstanding partnership. Egypt was the first country on the African continent to receive foreign aid from China during the 1950s (Morgan and Zheng, 2019a), as well as the first African country to recognize the People's Republic of China (in 1956). The two countries have in general remained close ever since. Egypt's Health Minister Hala Zayed had also visited China to show solidarity in March 2020, a gesture which China replayed by dispatching masks, other supplies, and later vaccines when COVID-19 hit Egypt (Xinhua, 2021e). It appears that this established partnership was sufficiently strong to encourage China to allocate substantial numbers of vaccines to the country despite few ostensible direct benefits to pandemic control at home or regional stability.

Alternative arguments

Those who view Chinese vaccine donations either as part of a strategic agenda of geopolitical competition to remake world order, or as an altruistic program freely available to all, could nonetheless rightly point out that in the early months of the global vaccine rollout China had pledged donations of vaccines to many more countries, including in Africa. For example, as early as March 2021, China's foreign ministry confirmed that Beijing had pledged donations to 80 countries and three international organizations (CGTN, 2021b).

Nonetheless, the empirical data show that in the initial months of the vaccine rollout, the bulk of Chinese vaccine donations went to China's neighbourhood and a small number of other strategic partners. Donations to other countries, including much of Africa, were largely in small numbers: sufficient to signal solidarity, and perhaps the promise of more once supplies were less constrained, but not to vaccinate substantial numbers of people.[6]

The author's data suggest that the average number of donated doses delivered to partners in the Global South as of the end of June 2021 was just over 170,000 per country, a tiny fraction of that required to vaccinate a substantial share of the population for most countries. A similar estimate of 200,000 is provided by other sources (Taylor, 2021). Nearby Asian states such as Cambodia, Pakistan, Laos and Nepal, on the other hand, had received approximately 2.8 million, 1.6 million, 1.1 million and 0.8 million doses, respectively.

As is discussed further in the concluding chapter, as supply of vaccines ramps up and the exchange of COVID-19 vaccines becomes a routine rather than a crisis based transaction, significant supplies of Chinese vaccines could be expected beyond its immediate neighbourhood. For example, President Xi Jinping's announcement of a commitment to donate 600 million doses of COVID-19 vaccines to the Africa at the Forum on China–Africa Cooperation (FOCAC) in November 2021 signals a rebalancing toward Africa, although it is not clear how quickly and to what extent these pledged doses have been delivered.

Nonetheless, during the initial months of the vaccine rollout – when the gap between supply and demand for vaccines was acute – the evidence strongly suggests that donations were guided by the imperative to control the pandemic in China's neighbourhood and mitigate the risk of imported infections, while at the same time seizing the opportunity to further ties with established strategic partners.

Following established aid practices

Given Beijing's long established practice of providing bilateral donations of medical goods and other medical support in response to health needs overseas described in the previous chapter, it would have been somewhat surprising if the Chinese government had not shipped vaccines overseas in response to COVID-19. China's vaccine donation practices likewise reflected the established modes of engagement with global health aid discussed in Chapter Two.

First, China principally offered donations on a bilateral rather than multilateral basis, following an agreement between the Chinese government and the recipient government. While a small number were given by the People's Liberation Army (PLA),[7] the vast majority were provided by the Chinese government and handed over via China's embassy networks. As the case of Myanmar below shows, the state affiliated Chinese Red Cross was also involved in providing vaccine donations in some cases. Nonetheless, there is little evidence of any large scale independent civil society involvement in donating or administering Chinese vaccines overseas.

Likewise, Chinese contributions to multilateral vaccine distribution initiatives were also limited compared to its bilateral efforts. COVAX is the leading multilateral mechanism for distributing vaccine doses to low- and middle-income countries, established by the WHO, the Coalition for Epidemic Preparedness Innovations (CEPI) and the Gavi vaccine alliance (CEPI, 2021). COVAX is both a mechanism for donations and a procurement facility. All major countries in Europe and North America, as well as China and India, signed up to contribute in 2020, although China's reluctance to engage multilaterally is exemplified by the fact that it did not sign up until 9 October 2020, after COVAX's own sign up deadline had passed the previous month (Adlakha, 2020). Indeed, while some Chinese firms have agreed commercial supply deals with COVAX, as of May 2022 the World Trade Organization and IMF (n.d.) COVID-19 vaccine trade tracker suggested that no country had received any donations of Chinese vaccines via COVAX. (By comparison, the author's data suggest that around 23 million bilateral donated doses were delivered by China during the first six months of 2021.)[8]

Moreover, as with most Chinese overseas aid, the Chinese government has turned largely, although not exclusively, to an SOE for procurement. According to the author's data almost 85 per cent of Chinese vaccine donations shipped overseas during the first half of 2021 were procured from the state owned Sinopharm. Meanwhile, just over 10 per cent of the government's donations to the Global South were procured from the private enterprise Sinovac, despite Sinovac (as is described in the next chapter) being the largest overall manufacturer of Chinese COVID-19 vaccines.[9] These trends are also corroborated by other data sources such as Beijing Bridge (n.d.), who put the proportion of total donations procured from Sinopharm at 60 per cent as of early 2022.

Illustrative case studies

This section illustrates the dynamics laid out in the preceding section through the case studies of Myanmar and Pakistan, which were both among China's top recipients of vaccine donations during the first half of 2021, but under different contexts. Pakistan is an extremely close diplomatic partner that also shares a border with the region of Xinjiang, in which the maintenance of stability is of paramount importance to the Communist Party. It was therefore naturally one of the first countries to receive donations from Beijing. The story of Chinese vaccine donations in Myanmar, on the other hand, is more unorthodox and complicated. After Myanmar's February 2021 coup delayed the implementation of earlier promises made to Aung San Suu Kyi, China's relations with the new military government stabilized and batches of donations arrived from May onwards. Nonetheless, as the analysis below details, concern about infections crossing over the Yunnan–Myanmar border were in fact sufficient to motivate China to reportedly take the unusual step of simultaneously donating vaccines to rebel groups in border regions.

Myanmar

Traditionally, China and Myanmar have a close but complicated relationship. In line with its broader approach to regional politics, Beijing's primary interest has long been stability (Ganesan, 2011). Myanmar's transition from military rule to a quasi-civilian government in 2011 complicated ties, as it brought increasing scrutiny within Myanmar on China's economic role in the country (Sun, 2012). Nonetheless, over time Beijing developed a strong and deep economic and political relationship, under the framework of the BRI, with the democratic government led by Aung San Suu Kyi. In what would be his last foreign visit before the start of the pandemic, Chinese President Xi Jinping visited Myanmar in January 2020. During the trip, China and Myanmar signed 32 BRI-related deals (Taylor, 2021). Reflecting their close ties, Chinese Foreign Minister Wang Yi promised vaccine aid to Aung San Suu Kyi during a visit in January 2021 (Reuters, 2021b; Mizzima, 2021).

However, the military coup that took place in Myanmar on 1 February of that year complicated the implementation of the Foreign Minister's promise. Experts reported that Beijing was unhappy with the development, given its potential to dislocate an otherwise solid economic and political relationship (Han, 2021). However, Beijing's interest in regional stability overrode any previous loyalties to Aung San Suu Kyi's government, and China's response to the coup was to call for stability and avoid overtly condemning the new military rule, and cooperate with the new government once it had been established (Zhabina, 2021).

As such, the January promise was eventually fulfilled in early May, when 500,000 Sinopharm doses were delivered to Yangon airport via the Chinese PLA. The choice to use the PLA to supply these doses likely reflects a desire to strengthen ties between Chinese and Myanmar military elites in the context of the key role of the military in Myanmar's government and society (Legarda, 2020). The delivery was also widely reported in Chinese state media and by the Chinese Embassy and other government departments (Xinhua, 2021b; China International Development Cooperation Agency, 2021; PRC Embassy in Myanmar, 2021).

However, around the same time an Aljazeera report appeared that stated that 20,000 people in Myanmar had already been 'quietly vaccinated' against COVID-19 by armed rebel groups (Lusan and Fishbein, 2021). Based on interviews with spokespeople for the Kachin Independence Organization rebel group, that same report stated that the Chinese-made Sinovac vaccines had been provided to the rebel groups by the Chinese Red Cross, a state affiliated organization, and administered by Chinese personnel, and that enough shipments to vaccinate the entire region were expected in future. The provision of vaccine donations by China to rebels in Myanmar was later confirmed by statements from spokespersons of rebel groups reported in multiple reliable international and regional media outlets (France24, 2021; The Irrawady, 2021; *South China Morning Post*, 2021; ASEAN Post, 2021), although it was not – to the best of the author's knowledge – mentioned by any Chinese state media organs.

This situation was unorthodox for two reasons: first, aiding of armed rebels (even if only through vaccines) appears to violate China's long professed principle of not getting involved in civil conflicts inside other states. Second, as mentioned earlier, Beijing was simultaneously providing the military government in Myanmar with COVID-19 vaccines. This raises the question of why Beijing was motivated to send vaccine donations to the rebel groups, especially given that, as Hong Kong University's Enze Han noted, Myanmar's military government 'definitely doesn't like [it]' (*The Straits Times*, 2021).

Importantly, some of the rebel controlled territories are located on the border between Myanmar and China's south-western province of Yunnan. Prior to the pandemic, the border was relatively porous, and Chinese authorities had struggled to control the coronavirus in those regions, despite officially sealing the border (the Chinese border city of Ruili is notorious within China for enduring some of the country's longest localized COVID-19 lockdowns (Wang and Dong, 2021)). In April 2021, Yunnan faced a substantial outbreak that led to the dismissal of the Ruili Party Secretary (Chick, 2021).

While China has continued to keep quiet on its seemingly unusual decision to donate vaccines to the rebels,[10] official statements about its parallel vaccine aid to Myanmar's government confirm that pandemic control in border regions is a motivation for donating vaccines to the country. In a press briefing on China's anti-coronavirus international cooperation, CIDCA's head Luo Zhaohui described providing vaccines to Myanmar as 'an effective mechanism to curb any cross-border spread of the virus' (State Council Information Office, 2021b). The state media outlet *China Daily* later reported that provision of vaccines to Myanmar was directly prompted by the economic and social impact of cross-border infections on Chinese border cities, with the dual goals of assisting China's neighbour and 'preventing imported infection in China' (*China Daily*, 2021). Likewise, in July 2021 Myanmar officials confirmed that priority access to donations of vaccines from the Chinese government would be given to residents living close to the border with China (ASEAN Post, 2021).

Key events in China's donations of vaccines to Myanmar during the first six months of 2021 are summarized in Table 3.2.

Throughout 2021, both Myanmar's government (Xinhua, 2021a) and rebel groups continued to receive Chinese-made doses (France24, 2021). Later that year, as both vaccine supplies and China's relations with Myanmar's new military regime

Table 3.2: Key events in Chinese vaccine donations to Myanmar, 1 January–30 June 2021

Date	Description
11 January 2021	Chinese Foreign Minister Wang Yi visits Myanmar and promises donations of Chinese COVID-19 vaccines to Aung San Suu Kyi's elected government.
1 February 2021	Military coup in Myanmar. China does not condemn the new government publicly, but is reportedly concerned about implications for stability.
April–early May 2021	Localized COVID-19 outbreak in Yunnan province on the border with Myanmar. Ruili city Party Secretary is dismissed as a result.
2 May 2021	500,000 doses of the Sinopharm vaccine donated by the Chinese government via the PLA arrive in Myanmar.
From May 2021	Various reports emerge of Chinese donations of vaccines to rebel groups in border regions via the state affiliated Chinese Red Cross.

Source: Compiled by author from own data and media reports.

stabilized, these initial donations paved the way both for commercial sales of both the Sinopharm and Sinovac vaccines, and for manufacturing deals for the production of Chinese-developed vaccines in Myanmar.

Vaccine donations from China have played a substantial role in Myanmar's domestic vaccination rollout. Data from the IMF-WHO (n.d.) COVID-19 Vaccine Supply Tracker indicated that as of the end of 2021, the country had secured enough doses to vaccinate 10 per cent of the country's population just through bilateral donations from China.

Nonetheless, while Chinese vaccine deliveries to Myanmar during the first half of 2021 were donated, in the latter half of the year commercial sales from Chinese manufacturers significantly overtook government donations, reflecting the

Table 3.3: Donations and sales of Chinese vaccines to Myanmar's government, 2021 (% of doses)

	1 January–30 June 2021	1 January–31 December 2021
Donations	100%	23%
Sales	0%	77%

Note: The data do not include doses provided to rebel groups.
Source: Compiled by author. Data up to 30 June 2021 are author's own data. Data up to end of 2021 are from Beijing Bridge (n.d.).[14]

broader trend in China's overseas vaccine supplies away from donations and toward commercial sales. Table 3.3 summarizes the share of donations and sales in Chinese-made vaccines acquired by the Myanmar government in 2021.

Pakistan

The fact that Pakistan received a large proportion of China's early COVID-19 vaccine donations should come as no surprise to those familiar with the relationship between the two neighbours, which are close traditional allies. China–Pakistan ties date back to 1951, when Pakistan became the first majority Muslim state to recognize the People's Republic of China. However, relations between the two countries were initially complicated by Pakistan's ties to the US and its membership of the anti-Communist Southeast Asia Treaty Organization (SEATO). Mutual mistrust of and conflict with India brought the two states together starting in the early 1960s (Khalid, 2021). Since then, their relations have been characterized by a remarkably stable 'complex interdependence' (Hussain et al, 2020). China first started to provide economic and military aid to Pakistan in the 1960s, and Pakistan was the first non-Communist country to operate direct flights to Beijing from 1963 (Ahmar, 2020). The relationship deepened further when Pakistan acted as a broker in facilitating the thaw in US–China relations in 1970 and 1971 (Khan, 2011).

More recently, Pakistan has become a focal point in China's BRI. The China–Pakistan Economic Corridor (CPEC) aims to develop land transport routes and pipeline connections from Xinjiang autonomous region in China to Pakistan's Gwadar port. For both sides, CPEC represents an opportunity to create an alternative to the Straits of Malacca, a maritime bottleneck. For China, it is also an opportunity to balance against India (Garlick, 2018), and to further improve relations with a country bordering its Xinjiang region, the stability of which is of paramount importance to Beijing. For Pakistan, it is a source of billions of dollars in infrastructure financing from Chinese state policy banks and commercial banks, with the potential to increase inward foreign direct investment (FDI) and trade.

As mentioned previously, during the initial coronavirus outbreak in Wuhan, Pakistan's president visited China in a demonstration of support. The joint communique issued at the end of the visit pointed to 'a singular expression of Pakistan's solidarity with its "iron brother"' (Xinhua, 2020a). Shortly after the visit, as the first wave of the virus spread around the world, China dispatched a medical team to Pakistan. Close economic and people-to-people ties continued throughout the COVID-19 crisis, as both sides have expressed an intention to 'march forward' with CPEC despite the pandemic (Wang, 2021). The fact that Pakistan was hit hard by COVID-19 in both health and economic terms (Shafi et al, 2020), coupled with the risks of corresponding social instability (Akhtar et al, 2021), created an added incentive for China to seize the opportunity to strengthen Sino-Pakistan ties through supporting its neighbour with vaccine donations.

Unlike China's porous southwestern borders, the geography of the China–Pakistan border means the risks of imported infection via land crossings are minimal.[11] Flights remained in operation between the two countries throughout most of the pandemic;[12] however, these flights were subject to the same quarantine systems applied to citizens of all countries arriving on any international flights. As such, the direct benefits to China in terms of domestic pandemic control from donating vaccines are indirect and relatively minor, compared to the case of Myanmar's highly porous land border. Instead, the key motivation lies in maintenance of regional stability and supporting a longstanding friend and partner.

The first set of 500,000 doses donated by the Chinese government arrived in Pakistan on 31 January 2021 – the very first batch of donated Chinese vaccines to arrive at their destination (State Council Information Office, 2021a). A handover ceremony with media in attendance was held the following day at Pakistan's Nur Khan Air Force Base, and included the Chinese Ambassador and Pakistan's foreign and health ministers as well as various other officials (PRC Embassy in Pakistan, 2021a).

That first set of half a million donated doses was followed by subsequent batches of Sinopharm vaccines in February, March, April, May, and June 2021, both from the Chinese government and the PLA (PRC Embassy in Pakistan, 2021b). At the same time, as is discussed in more detail in the next chapter, Pakistan's government purchased vaccines on a commercial basis from Sinopharm, Sinovac and CanSino (whose clinical trials it had agreed to host). Over time, these commercial deals, which are the focus of the following chapter, dwarfed official donations. Pakistan also became one of the first countries to begin manufacturing Chinese-developed vaccines. A locally produced version of the CanSino vaccine (called 'PakVac') was launched in early June 2021, with the intention of mass provision for the local market (Shahzad, 2021; Siddiqui et al, 2021).

Table 3.4 below summarizes key events in China's supply of vaccines to Pakistan up to June 2021, while Figure 3.2 charts the rapid overtaking of official donations by commercial sales in Chinese vaccine deliveries to Pakistan from March of that year.

Table 3.4: Key events in Chinese vaccine donations to Pakistan, 1 January–30 June 2021

Date	Description
31 January 2021	Pakistan receives first batch of 500,000 Sinopharm vaccine doses from the Chinese government. They were the first donations of Chinese vaccines delivered overseas.
7 February 2021	The Pakistani armed forces become the first foreign armed forces to receive vaccine donations from China's PLA.
From March 2021 onward	Regular batches of both donated and commercially supplied Chinese vaccines arrive in Pakistan. Commercial sales begin to outstrip donations.
1 June 2021	Locally produced version of CanSino vaccine ('PakVac') launched in Pakistan.

Source: Compiled by author from own data and media reports.

Figure 3.2: Donations and sales of Chinese vaccines delivered to Pakistan, 1 January–30 June 2021 (number of doses, millions)

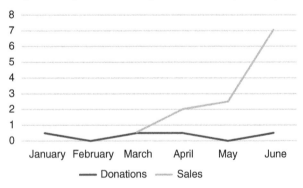

Source: Compiled by author from own data.[15]

Conclusion

In sum, the empirical evidence suggests that the Chinese government's vaccine donations during the first six months of 2021 were driven neither by a strategic attempt to reshape the global order, nor an altruistic program for the world's neediest. Instead, Chinese vaccine donations were mainly sent to countries in China's neighbourhood and/or those with which it had strong pre-existing relations.

There are three main interrelated reasons for this neighbourhood focus, two of which are primarily rooted in domestic rather than international politics. First of all, the Chinese party-state relies on performance legitimacy – the (perception of) effective governance – to justify its rule, and strict pandemic control domestically has become central to that legitimacy in the age of COVID-19 (Jing, 2021). As such, Chinese officials faced a pressing need to control the pandemic in China's border regions and thereby mitigate the risk of infections imported from abroad. Second, and relatedly, a stable regional environment and stable border regions are also important to the party-state's performance legitimacy. Assisting pandemic control in neighbouring states aimed to contribute to ensuring a stable environment for economic growth, and the party-state's continued legitimacy at home. Third, and also relatedly, due to its longstanding emphasis on regional stability China has worked hard to build relationships with countries in its neighbourhood (albeit with varying degrees of success). Vaccine donations therefore presented an opportunity to bolster relationships with existing allies while simultaneously contributing to pandemic control and stability.

The cases of Myanmar and Pakistan illustrate all of these dynamics, although with different emphases. Given Myanmar's porous border with China, mitigation of imported infections was paramount, to the extent that China found itself simultaneously donating vaccines to the government and to opposition rebel groups in control of border regions. Donations to Pakistan, on the other hand, were principally motivated by the goals of ensuring regional stability and bolstering relations with a key ally.

Myanmar and Pakistan share one important similarity: in both cases, while Chinese vaccine deliveries started with donations, these were later dwarfed by commercial sales (Pakistan from March 2021, Myanmar later in the year). This reflects the broader pattern mentioned in Chapter One: while China's vaccine donations have received substantial international attention – both positive and negative – the vast majority of Chinese vaccine supplies to the Global South have been sold on a commercial basis, rather than donated. Contextualizing, charting and explaining these commercial sales is the focus of the following chapter.

FOUR

Market Forces and Commercial Chinese Vaccine Sales

As the previous chapter described, the Chinese government's international donations of COVID-19 vaccines have garnered substantial attention, both positive and negative. However, discussions of China's role in the distribution of vaccines often fail to observe[1] that the vast majority of Chinese vaccine doses shipped abroad are not donations but commercial sales. The author's data indicate that of the Chinese-made doses delivered to the Global South during the first six months of 2021, around 90 per cent were commercial sales, and just 10 per cent donated.[2] Unpacking the forces driving these sales is therefore crucial to understanding overall Chinese vaccine supplies. This chapter describes and explains patterns in commercial deliveries of Chinese vaccines overseas during the first six months of 2021, when Chinese exporters Sinovac, Sinopharm and CanSino were some of the few players (alongside AstraZeneca) shipping substantial numbers of doses to low- and middle-income states.

The first section provides an overview of the world COVID-19 vaccine marketplace during the initial rollout of vaccines, and situates China within it. The second section describes how Chinese firms were able to seize the opportunity of the pandemic to boost their position in global vaccine markets, in part thanks to their linkages with and support from the state. The third second section maps the distribution of vaccines sold by Chinese manufacturers during the first six months of 2021. The distribution of vaccines sales indicates that they were driven by two factors: first, market forces, and specifically by the classic 'gravity' model, in which trade is correlated with economic size and distance; and second, clinical trial partnerships between purchasing countries and Chinese vaccine companies, which turned to overseas partners to test the efficacy of their new products due to low case numbers in China.

The world COVID-19 vaccine marketplace

Customers from the Global North dominated the demand side of the market for COVID-19 vaccines during the initial global vaccine rollout. Up to mid-2021,[3] of the total vaccine doses around the world agreed or in negotiation via commercial purchasing deals with manufacturers, two thirds involved high-income purchaser states, while around 16 per cent involved middle-income purchasers and just five per cent involved low-income purchasers.[4] As Figure 4.1 illustrates, the commercial supply of vaccines to high-income countries reflected the status quo described in Chapter Two: it was dominated by a relatively small set of large North American and European manufacturers, with an extremely limited role for Chinese companies.

Vaccinating the Global South

Although Global South countries were strongly disadvantaged relative to the Global North, some were able to secure vaccine deals, principally with Chinese firms and/or producers of the vaccine developed by UK-Swedish firm AstraZeneca in partnership with the UK's Oxford University, which is manufactured both by AstraZeneca and the SII. Of the commercial deals agreed or in negotiation by low- and middle-income states in mid-2021, just under one quarter of doses involved Chinese firms, while just over one quarter involved

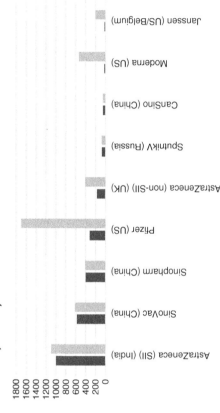

Figure 4.1: Deliveries of bilateral commercial vaccine deals by manufacturer to end-2021 (number of doses, millions)

Notes: The IMF and WHO track the aggregate delivery of vaccines by contract. The figure is calculated from data updated as of 5 January 2022, and so may include a small number of doses that were actually delivered in 2022. Unlike those made by other manufacturers which typically require two doses for a standard course, the CanSino and Janssen vaccines require only one dose to be considered 'fully vaccinated'.

Source: Compiled by author using data from the IMF-WHO COVID-19 Contracts & Donations Delivery Tracker (IMF and WHO, n.d.).

the AstraZeneca vaccine, with the remainder split between other vaccines.[5]

Figure 4.1 charts vaccine doses shipped and delivered under bilateral commercial deals to the Global South, and to countries of all income groups up to the end of 2021.

These data suggest that by the end of 2021, AstraZeneca / the SII and the three main Chinese manufacturers had each delivered just over 1 billion doses to the Global South, with a small number of doses provided by other suppliers, including Pfizer and Russia's Gamaleya Research Institute, which developed the SputnikV vaccine.

AstraZeneca / the SII's large volume of sales to the Global South is not surprising: AstraZeneca is one of the largest pharmaceutical companies in the world, and the Serum Institute is the world's largest maker of vaccines (Garrison, 2020). Conversely, neither Sinopharm, Sinovac nor CanSino were well known as major international vaccine exporters prior to the pandemic. As the following section details, while each had produced some vaccines for overseas and/or domestic markets prior to COVID-19, it was the pandemic that allowed these companies to seize the opportunity to become key players in the world vaccine marketplace.

Not a 'cheap' alternative, but an accessible one

Before proceeding, a clarification on pricing is needed. Chinese- and Indian-made vaccines are often assumed to be 'cheap alternatives' to those produced by manufacturers in North America and Europe (Haseltine, 2021). Reliable data on the pricing of COVID-19 vaccines are difficult to come by, given that pricing agreements between buyers and manufacturers are often kept confidential. However, data from UNICEF's (n.d.) COVID-19 vaccine market dashboard, which tracks any publicly reported prices of vaccine sales across all manufacturers, suggests the low cost assumption holds in the Indian case but not in the Chinese one.

Figure 4.2: Mean reported price per dose of COVID-19 vaccine paid by countries of the Global South, to end-2021 (US$)

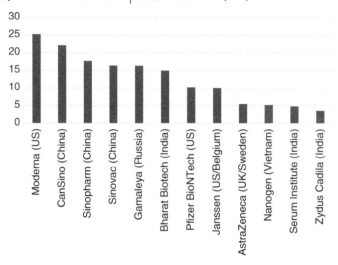

Notes: Does not include vaccines produced by Chinese developers sold in/to China, or prices paid by countries of the Global North. Data reflect only average publicly reported prices, actual price paid by individual countries depends on agreement between the manufacturer and purchaser, and may differ from the public reports tracked by UNICEF.
Source: Compiled by author using data from UNICEF's (n.d.) 'COVID-19 Vaccine Market Dashboard' as of 1 January 2022.

Figure 4.2 graphs the mean reported price per dose of COVID-19 vaccine paid by countries of the Global South up to the end of 2021. AstraZeneca and the Serum Institute's vaccines were among the lowest priced at around US$5 per dose, in part reflecting AstraZeneca's initial commitment not to profit from COVID-19 vaccines (Kuchler, 2021). Average prices per dose of reported agreements with Sinopharm, Sinovac and CanSino are US$18, US$16, and US$22 respectively (although CanSino's vaccine requires only one dose for a standard course and is therefore the least expensive of the three). Statements from CanSino representatives also suggest that the company practices tiered pricing, charging richer customers more (McGregor, 2021a).

Readers might wonder why financially constrained low- and middle-income countries chose comparatively expensive Sinovac, Sinopharm or CanSino vaccines when placed next to the cheaper AstraZeneca alternative. A critical reason is that it is doses actually shipped and administered to residents that contribute to addressing public health crises, not commitments or contracts. With the pandemic largely under control at home, China allowed its manufacturers to ship substantial numbers of doses to their overseas customers during the first half of 2021. It did not face the same pressure to take the extraordinary defensive steps taken by many other countries with COVID-19 vaccine manufacturing capabilities, such as export bans (which defy the normal rules of the game in international trade) and/ or buying up as much of their manufacturers' supply as possible.

On the other hand, during the first six months of 2021, multiple forces hampered shipments of AstraZeneca shots.[6] These included technical production problems in some factories (Weaver, 2021), contract terms that stipulated that certain customers – including the EU and the UK – should be supplied first (BBC News, 2021), concerns about rare blood clotting side effects (Mueller, 2021), and export restrictions in India (Beaumont, 2021; Burke et al, 2021). The latter was particularly problematic for countries of the Global South that had ordered AstraZeneca doses made by the Serum Institute, as India's export ban – instituted in response to the devastating wave of the Delta variant at home – lasted from April to November 2021. Richer countries' pre-orders of vaccines sold by AstraZeneca and other manufacturers meant that Global South countries seeking to buy doses that could be delivered quickly, and therefore rapidly administered to citizens, turned to Sinovac, Sinopharm and CanSino.[7]

'Seizing the opportunity' of the pandemic

COVID-19 has presented a commercial opportunity for pharmaceutical firms around the world.[8] At least 40 pharmaceutical and/or healthcare industry bosses have become billionaires, including in China, Europe and the US (Tognini, 2021). All major manufacturers of vaccine candidates approved for use in 2020 or 2021 have generated substantial revenues as a result of their scientific success, although AstraZeneca and Janssen initially promised not to profit from COVID-19 vaccines (Sung et al, 2021). For example, a study by the People's Vaccine Alliance, a movement of NGOs, public health experts, economists and religious leaders, found that Pfizer, its partner BioNTech and Moderna are estimated to have made combined pre-tax profits of US$34 billion in 2021, a significant increase on previous years in large part due to their COVID-19 vaccines (Oxfam, 2021).

Likewise, Chinese vaccine developers have gained substantially, albeit from a much weaker initial position in international vaccine markets than giants like AstraZeneca, Janssen and Pfizer. Sinopharm's profits in the 2020–21 fiscal year were up 38 per cent compared to the previous year (Fortune, 2022). Sinovac reported a net income in the first half of 2021 of US$8.6 billion, having made a net loss of US$8.7 million over the same period in the previous year (Nasdaq, 2021). CanSino, meanwhile, reported its first ever profit during the first half of 2021, thanks largely to its COVID-19 vaccine (Bloomberg, 2021).

China's key players

As described in Chapter Two, the Chinese pharmaceutical sector was relatively underperforming compared to its equivalent in other major economies prior to the pandemic, and its main vaccine developers were largely unknown outside of China. As of the time of writing, six Chinese firms[9] have developed vaccines approved for use within China, with several additional firms with candidates at various stages of development (Basta and Moodie, n.d.). However, two companies dominated the initial global and domestic rollout of vaccines in 2021: state owned Sinopharm and private company Sinovac, with

CanSino, also a private company, providing a smaller but not insignificant number of doses. The following paragraphs briefly contextualize and review the history of these three firms.

Sinopharm

China National Pharmaceutical Group, commonly known as Sinopharm, is the oldest and most established of the three. It is a central level SOE, directly supervised by the SASAC, the government organ responsible for overseeing central SOEs. Sinopharm does business across the medical and healthcare sector, including production and distribution of multiple types of drugs for non-communicable and communicable diseases, vaccines, retail, healthcare and traditional Chinese medicine.

Typical of many Chinese central SOEs, Sinopharm is a vast entity with over 1,100 subsidiaries (and subsidiaries of subsidiaries) of various origins and specializations. China National Biotec Group (CNBG), the subsidiary that produced the COVID-19 vaccines, dates back to 1919, when it was created as the National Epidemic Prevention Bureau of the Beiyang Republican government. After the founding of the People's Republic in 1949, it was subsumed under the Ministry of Health, with the CNBG incorporated in 1988 alongside broader economic reforms that saw many branches of the government restructured into SOEs.[10]

Until 2009, however, the Sinopharm parent company was insolvent and struggling. Its successful expansion during the 2010s was kickstarted by Song Zhiping, its chairman from 2009 to April 2014 (Zhang, 2021, p 217). A high profile business leader, Song drove forward market reforms, almost immediately listing part of the business on the Hong Kong Stock Exchange (Reuters, 2009). The restructuring was a representation of Song's well publicized formula of 'strength of central enterprises plus the flexibility of private enterprises' (iAsk, 2016). Sinopharm joined the *Fortune* 500 rankings of the world's largest companies in 2013 (*Fortune*, 2022).

Sinopharm has a well-established position in domestic vaccine markets in China. According to the company's website, it supplies over 80 per cent of the vaccines used in the country's Expanded Program on Immunization, its flagship program for immunizing children from vaccine-preventable diseases (Sinopharm, n.d.). The Chengdu arm of CNBG produced the Japanese Encephalitis vaccine that was the first Chinese-made vaccine to receive WHO prequalification (Parry, 2014). However, vaccines remained a small part of its overseas business until COVID-19 (Douglas and Samant, 2018; Shepherd and Gross, 2021).

Sinovac

Sinovac is a private enterprise and is much smaller and younger than Sinopharm. It was founded in 2001 in Beijing's Haidian district, with offices in Peking University Biological Park, a cluster zone for biotech enterprises developed by the local government and located in China's top higher education institution. As the company name suggests, Sinovac was created specifically with the aim of producing vaccines.

Its key founders, Yin Weidong and Pan Aihua, are both scientists. According to an account published by Peter Halesworth (2021), a US businessman who worked with the company for seven years, CEO Yin was a young entrepreneur with a promising vaccine for hepatitis A but in need of capital to commercialize it, while Pan was a professor who could provide connections and bring in money.

In 2002, Yin's hepatitis A vaccine was launched commercially. The hepatitis vaccine was approved for domestic use in China in 2005, and included in the national vaccination programme three years later (McGregor, 2021b). The company also developed a SARS vaccine in response to the 2002–03 crisis, which reached phase one trials (although this appeared – initially – to be a poor investment when the outbreak died out) as well as vaccines for other diseases including influenza.

The company is listed on the US NASDAQ stock exchange, although trading in Sinovac shares was halted by the exchange in 2019, an development that Seeking Alpha (2021) reports is the result of a dispute arose when a group of unhappy stakeholders, including Pan, tried to take control of the firm from CEO Yin.

The dispute did not stop the firm securing WHO preapproval for its hepatitis A vaccine in 2017. Prior to COVID-19, Sinovac had continued to develop new products and make some strides into international markets. It started to export the hepatitis vaccine to Mongolia in 2009, and a flu vaccine to the Philippines that same year. It sells both of these products in Asia and the broader Global South (Sinovac, n.d.). Nonetheless, it remained a relatively small, niche firm on the global stage. Its total sales in 2019, for example, were US$246 million, or just over 1 per cent of AstraZeneca's sales in that same year (Businesswire, 2020; SEC, 2021).

CanSino

CanSino was founded in 2009 by Yu Xuefeng, a Chinese-born scientist who had studied and worked in Canada for two decades, alongside collaborators Zhu Tao, Qiu Dongxu and Mao Huihua. A promising young graduate of China's prestigious Nankai University in the northern city of Tianjin, Yu entered McGill University's PhD programme in 1991. After gaining his PhD, he worked at the vaccine company Sanofi Pasteur in Canada (Hurby, 2017).

Yu was reportedly ultimately drawn back to China by a sense of duty and the country's lucrative support via the 'Thousand Talents Programme', part of China's efforts to develop a more innovation oriented economic model (Hurby, 2017). However, he reportedly retained ties with Canada, and the 'Can' in the company's name is in fact a reference to the time spent in Canada by Yu and his collaborators (Cohen, 2020).

Like Sinovac's founders, Yu and his cofounders located the company in a local government development zone that aimed to foster innovation, in line with the country's broader economic strategy. Returning to the city of Yu's alma mater, they selected the Tianjin Economic-Technological Development Area (TEDA), in the city's Binhai New Area.

Prior to COVID-19, the company's only vaccine to receive international approval was one against Ebola, developed in 2014. That vaccine had been developed in collaboration with Canada's National Research Council (NRC), using technology licensed from the latter (Pinkerton, 2021). The success of the Ebola vaccine led to substantial investment from local and foreign investors (Hurby, 2017). Buoyed by the success of its Ebola vaccine, CanSino became the first vaccine company to be listed on the Hong Kong Stock Exchange in 2019, in a US$160 million IPO (Paul Hastings LLP, 2019).

However, as mentioned earlier, the company did not actually make a profit until the COVID-19 pandemic, which made it 'the hottest stock in Hong Kong', according to *Fortune* magazine (Yu, 2020). As Yu Xuefeng presciently predicted in an interview with the Shanghai-based publication *Sixth Tone* in 2017, '[i]f you can make one blockbuster product … you completely change the market' (Hurby, 2017). Sinopharm, Sinovac and CanSino did indeed shake up global vaccine markets during the pandemic, but as the section below details, they were each helped along the way by collaborations with the state.

State–corporate cooperation in vaccine development

Manufacturers across China, Europe, Russia, the US and elsewhere developed their COVID-19 vaccines at unprecedented speed, thanks in part to government support. Indeed, AstraZeneca, Janssen, Pfizer-BioNTech and Moderna all received funding from either the US government, the UK government, or both (Wouters et al, 2021).

Nonetheless, state–corporate linkages were particularly important in the Chinese cases. Hu and Chen (2021) describe Chinese COVID-19 vaccine development as a 'state-driven collaborative model', in which innovation occurs through a combination of state mobilization and private sector incentives. According to Hu and Chen, this has three key features: alleviating the risks of taking a bet on a new product through public investment; strategically directing resources; and sharing and integrating information.

First, with respect to funding, because of the government's pre-existing framework for building a more innovative economy described in Chapter Two, it already had multiple mechanisms and schemes for supporting scientific research, which could be quickly reoriented toward coronavirus vaccines. China's MOST swiftly directed national level research programmes toward COVID-19 vaccine research from January 2020 (Winch et al, 2021). As a result, researchers in China quickly noticed an increase in the frequency and amount of grant funding available in this field (Murphy, 2020).

Second, in January 2020, a coordination group was established under the State Council (the top government organ, equivalent to the Cabinet in the UK) comprised of 13 relevant ministries (Winch et al, 2021). Likewise, in mid-February 2020, a COVID-19 vaccine task force comprised of senior officials from key departments, including MOST, was established (Hu and Chen, 2021). These mechanisms facilitated both strategic direction of resources to vaccine developers and information sharing.

In addition, as discussed in more detail below, Sinovac and CanSino – both relatively small firms lacking the centralized heft of Sinopharm – were able to leverage specific partnerships with other central and/or local actors with which they had pre-existing relationships. As a result, all three firms were able to move through the three stages of clinical trials[11] and bring their vaccines to market at speed.

Sinopharm: The state takes the lead

On 19 January 2020, Sinopharm's vaccine subsidiary CNBG developed a 'leading small group' in response to the outbreak centred on Wuhan (CNBG, 2021). At the time, the novel coronavirus was yet to be named, but the company had already tasked its researchers with exploring both inactivated and genetically engineered vaccines, according to Sinopharm-CNBG Chairman Yang Xiaoming (SASAC, 2020b).

By 1 February 2020 (one week after the lockdown of Wuhan), the company already had approval from the MOST for undertaking an 'emergency project' into vaccine R&D (SASAC, 2021b). The sums involved were substantial: according to a report on vaccine development published by the SASAC in April 2020, by that point the company had arranged for RMB1 billion yuan (around US$160 million) in support for vaccine development (SASAC, 2020a).

As a central SOE, Sinopharm also benefitted from the coordinating role of the SASAC. On 10 February, the SASAC Party Secretary Hao Peng held a videoconference connecting several key SOEs, including Sinopharm, together to urge them to make use of their respective comparative advantages in tackling the outbreak of the new virus, as well as to work with academic research institutes (SASAC, 2020c).

Sinopharm-CNBG quickly launched into testing vaccines on animals (Wang et al, 2020). The process was accelerated by testing the vaccines on multiple animals at once, rather than moving through different species one by one (SASAC, 2020a). The Wuhan branch of Sinopharm-CNBG obtained approval for accelerated stage 1 and 2 clinical trials from the State Food and Drug Administration, which had opened a 'green channel' of simultaneous reviews to speed vaccine-related approvals, on 12 April 2020, with the Beijing branch securing similar approvals on 28 April 2020. At the same time as getting started on human trials, the Beijing based team was already preparing the technical documents required for the WHO to approve the vaccine for emergency use (SASAC, 2021c).

Simultaneously, the company ramped up production capacity, facilitated by government administrative support. An article published by the SASAC on the completion of

Sinopharm–CNBG's first new COVID-19 vaccine factory in Beijing in August 2020 points to the support of the Beijing municipal government as a key reason why the factory's construction could be completed in only two months. It also credits the swift organization of biosafety inspections to the relevant national level government departments (SASAC, 2020d). At the time, the factory was the world's largest production facility for inactivated COVID-19 vaccines (although the company has since built several more).

Vaccine development work in the Wuhan branch of CNBG was complicated by the city's status as the epicentre of the outbreak in China, which resulted in non-local employees who had returned to their hometowns for Chinese New Year being shut out outside of quarantine borders. Some workers were able to return with special dispensation, and one non-local staffer in vaccine quality control was even helped back by the conductor of a high speed train who made a special stop in Wuhan after learning what her job was and why she was trying to get in to the city (SASAC, 2020a).

An unusually colourful (for Chinese official communications) profile of manager Xu Zhihong published by the SASAC in early 2021 gives an insight into the day-to-day practicalities of this 'wartime speed' (SASAC, 2021a). According to Xu, a storage and transportation manager in Sinopharm's Beijing based team, he and his colleagues worked through weekends and slept in the office. His account describes being stuck in cold temperatures (which the doses require to stay effective) for days, and domestic logistical challenges such as airplane delays because of China's strict anti-pandemic measures. When the company moved to phase three trials, which were conducted overseas, Xu also describes his battle to develop special boxes to maintain the vaccines at the required low temperatures in hot weather countries in the Middle East, North Africa and Latin America.

Indeed, while all three manufacturers conducted the early stages of trials in China, when the time came for the third and final stage, there were insufficient COVID-19 case numbers within the country to conduct studies on vaccine efficacy, which necessitated going abroad. Sinopharm and its fellow Chinese vaccine makers had to quickly find international partners. Crucially, the countries that had both the willingness and the healthcare infrastructure to host trials were able to secure priority access to sales of their Chinese partner's product.[12]

Morocco, for example, signed two cooperation agreements on stage 3 trials with Sinopharm-CNBG in August 2020 (MAP, 2020). The cooperation agreements were signed between Morocco's Ministry of Health and CNBG representatives rather than the Chinese government, although Morocco's Foreign Minister Nasser Bourita referred to the longstanding cooperative relationship between the two countries, and to the strategic partnership concluded in 2016 between Morocco and Beijing, when describing the signing of the deal (Morocco Ministry of Foreign Affairs, 2020). The agreements specifically granted the country privileged access to Sinopharm's vaccines once the trials were concluded, and over the longer term included technology transfer and the setup of Sinopharm manufacturing facilities in Morocco (El Azami, 2021). As a result of these agreements, Morocco was Sinopharm's largest Global South customer during the first half of 2021, with over one third of the company's delivered commercial exports going to the country.

Sinopharm-CNGB's Beijing branch received domestic approval for its COVID-19 vaccine on 30 December 2020 (CNBG, 2021), with the candidate from the Wuhan branch receiving approval in February 2021. As Figure 4.1 illustrates, measured by deliveries of commercial bilateral deals, by the end of 2021 Sinopharm was the third largest vaccine exporter to the Global South (second only to AstraZeneca / the SII and Sinovac), and the fifth largest overall in the world. In short, the pandemic has greatly increased Sinopharm's position in global vaccine markets, and – correspondingly – the company's profits. While the firm ranked 169th in the *Fortune* 500 list of the world's largest companies in 2019, it had climbed to 109th by early 2022, thanks in large part to COVID-19 vaccines (*Fortune*, 2022).

On the one hand, this success was surprising, given China's former relative weakness in international vaccine markets. On the other hand, the fact that Sinopharm, a central SOE, vaccine giant domestically, and major global player in healthcare more generally, emerged as one of China's key COVID-19 vaccine providers is not unexpected. More surprising is the rapid expansion of the comparatively unknown private enterprises Sinovac and CanSino, discussed in the following sections.

Sinovac: Leveraging an eclectic mix of private and public support

The resources Sinovac had put into the development of a vaccine against SARS in 2002–03 proved extremely useful after COVID-19 came along. As Sinovac CEO Yin Weidong told *TIME* magazine, the two viruses are 'like brothers', and as a result Yin and his staff were able to get a head start (Campbell, 2020). By 20 April 2020, the team had published provisional results showing the vaccine candidate was safe and effective in mice, rats and rhesus monkeys (Gao et al, 2020). The study was funded by the MOST as a National Key Research and Development Programme, and also by the Thousand Talents Program and the Natural Science Foundation of China. Human phase one and two trials started in China in April 2020.

While the company originally started out with the aim of developing vaccines to deal with the outbreak in Wuhan, by the summer of 2020 Sinovac had reoriented its ambitions internationally, according to CEO Yin, to 'face the world' (McNeil, 2020).

Sinovac secured support from an eclectic mix of local government and private sources, in addition to central government funding, to facilitate its vaccine development and expansion of production capacity. In April 2020, the company obtained 70,000 square metres of land for a new manufacturing complex from the Daxing district government in Beijing, alongside a low interest credit line of US$7.5 million from the Bank of Beijing (Liu and Goh, 2020). In May 2020, it announced that it had secured US$15 million in loans from Advantech Capital, a Chinese private equity fund, and Vivo Capital, a Californian healthcare investment firm, to support its COVID-19 vaccine work (Sinovac, 2020b). In December of that year, it secured a further US$500 million for expansion of manufacturing capacity from a Chinese investor, Sino Biopharmaceutical Limited. CEO Yin stated that this funding would help the company 'improve our vaccine sales capabilities, [and] expand in Asia [sic] markets' (Sinovac, 2020c).

Like Sinopharm, Sinovac had to seek out overseas partners for phase three trials. The first such trials took place in Brazil, Indonesia and Turkey, countries that CEO Yin said were chosen because of their large populations, COVID-19 prevalence and limited domestic R&D abilities (McNeil, 2020). The collaboration with Brazil's Instituto Butantan, a São Paulo state government institute, was announced on 11 June 2020. According to Sinovac's press release, the deal was a means of ensuring access to the vaccine for Brazil's people, and was intended to pave the way both for the commercialization of the product in Brazil – a major emerging economy – and also for development of local manufacturing facilities for the vaccine (Sinovac, 2020a). Likewise, the cooperation deals with Indonesia and Turkey paved the way for early access to Sinovac's vaccine for those countries, although the initial large scale shipments to the latter were delayed for unknown reasons (Sinovac, 2020d; Reuters, 2021c).

While Sinovac's vaccine has been subject to speculations about efficacy (in brief, the data suggest it *does* meet the WHO's efficacy standards, although it is not as effective as several other vaccines in widespread use around the world), it has been an unquestionable success in terms of distribution and revenues. According to the author's data, almost three quarters of Chinese vaccine doses delivered to the Global South during the first six months of 2021 were made by Sinovac. As shown in Figure 4.1, throughout 2021 it remained the largest Chinese supplier of vaccines overseas, significantly surpassing its much larger state owned cousin, as well as most manufacturers from other countries.

CanSino: Private–military partnership

On 29 February 2020, 11 days before COVID-19 was declared a pandemic by the WHO, and three weeks before the United Kingdom went into lockdown, Dr Chen Wei – a 54-year old PLA Major General – and six of her team of scientists, became some of the first people on the planet to receive an experimental COVID-19 vaccination.

An epidemiologist and virologist by training, Chen is a leading researcher at China's Academy of Military Medical Sciences, a scientific branch of the Chinese PLA. In recent years, China has stepped up medical research within the military as part of wider PLA efforts to modernize and increase collaboration with civilian institutions (a strategy known as 'military-civil fusion') (Lewis, 2020).[13] Chen's team – working out of the then-coronavirus epicentre of Wuhan – was partnering with CanSino on the new vaccine (Cohen, 2020). The collaboration between the military scientists and the ambitious private enterprise had its roots in Major General Chen's work with CanSino in the development of the company's Ebola vaccine (Greeven, 2020).

CanSino had started contemplating making COVID-19 vaccines just a month and a half earlier than Dr Chen's test inoculation, after the genetic sequence of the virus had been made available on 11 January 2020. However, according to CEO Yu Xuefeng, the company hesitated at first, remembering that corporations (like Sinovac) that put a lot of money into developing SARS vaccines in response to the 2002–03 outbreak got their fingers burned when the disease died out (Cohen,

2020). However, by Chinese New Year in late January 2020, after the lockdown of the city of Wuhan, the company was working flat out on vaccine development. It started conducting accelerated animal trials in February, before injecting Dr Chen and her colleagues at the end of that month (CGTN, 2020).

Phase one human trials started shortly afterwards in March 2020 in Wuhan, with the first results – which indicated that the vaccine was safe and merited further investigation – published in *The Lancet* medical journal in May 2020, the first phase one trial results published in the world (Zhu, Li et al, 2020). Phase two trials, also in Wuhan, began shortly afterwards in April 2020, with the first findings – also promising – published in *The Lancet* in July (Zhu, Guan et al, 2020). Both trials were funded by the National Key R&D Programme of China (funded by MOST) and as a National Science and Technology Major Project, as well as by CanSino itself.

Because the Chinese military has its own medical approvals processes, CanSino and the PLA were also able to get their vaccine candidate cleared for military use more quickly than through waiting for the phase three trials to conclude (Cha and Kim, 2020). The vaccine was approved by the Central Military Commission on 25 June 2020 (Reuters, 2020). CEO Yu Xuefeng disclosed in a TV interview with state media channel CGTN (2020) in September of that year that the vaccine had already been distributed to Chinese peacekeepers working in regions of the world where the virus was circulating widely.

Alongside developing the vaccine in collaboration with the Chinese military, Yu also drew on his experiences and contacts from his former home of Canada. The company's vaccine was developed using technology that was originally produced by Canada's NRC, and Yu had originally hoped to undertake phase three clinical trials of the vaccine in Canada. However, the deal between CanSino and the Canadian government broke down because Chinese customs officials held up a shipment of the trial doses (Pinkerton, 2021). Yu attributed this setback to 'bureaucracy', but it is possible it was also a consequence of the deteriorating political relations between the two countries resulting from Canada's house arrest of Huawei CFO Meng Wenzhou and China's tit-for-tat arrest of two Canadian citizens (Jensen, 2020).

Unable to get customs approval to ship doses to its trial in Canada, the company turned to Argentina, Chile, Mexico, Pakistan and Russia to start phase three trials. According to the company's senior vice president for international business, these locations were chosen because they were 'places with viral circulation', and had 'infrastructure in place in the country, like hospitals, that was used to running immunization clinics and reporting trial data' (McGregor, 2021a). The phase three trial began in Pakistan in September 2020, in November in Mexico, and in December in Argentina, Chile and Russia, with around 45,000 volunteers participating across all five countries (Halperin et al, 2022).

However, the company was relatively slow to win broader regulatory approval, a fact that it attributed to its smaller size and limited experience with regulatory affairs, compared to Sinopharm and Sinovac, as well as the fact that CanSino's vaccine was based on newer viral vector technology that would require more scrutiny (McGregor, 2021a). Because of the regulatory delays, despite CanSino being the first company to start injecting the vaccine into humans, according to the author's data, only 2.5 per cent of Chinese vaccine doses delivered to the Global South during the first six months of 2021 were made by CanSino. As with Sinopharm and Sinovac, participation in clinical trials paved the way for access. The initial deliveries went exclusively to the first two clinical trial partners: Mexico and Pakistan.

In April 2021, the company held a ceremony for the opening of a new manufacturing centre for COVID-19 vaccines. Like the company's headquarters, the facility is located in Tianjin's TEDA zone in Binhai New Area. It is unclear what assistance, if any, the local government provided for the new facility beyond the pre-existing support packages for investment in the TEDA economic zone. However, Major General Chen Wei, alongside Binhai Party Secretary Lian Maojun, spoke at the ceremony. Chen pointed to the commercial-military collaboration as fulfilling societal responsibilities, while Lian pointed to the importance of biomanufacturing innovation to industry in the district (CanSino, 2021).

Despite playing a relatively small role in the initial global vaccine rollout, the company has big ambitions. It has published early stage trial data for a nasal spray version of its vaccine (which its scientists say may be better at triggering immune responses in the areas in which the virus infects the body) (Wu, Huang et al, 2021). As discussed further in the concluding chapter, CanSino is also working on an mRNA vaccine, which was cleared for clinical trials in early April 2022 (Reuters, 2022). Yu Xuefeng and his cofounders, meanwhile, join the Moderna and BioNTech CEOs in becoming billionaires as a result of COVID-19 vaccines (Tognini, 2021).

Overall, data suggest that the state–corporate collaboration has been successful in seizing the opportunity of the pandemic to advance China's position in global vaccine markets. According to the WTO-IMF COVID-19 Vaccine Trade Tracker (n.d.), as of the end of 2021, China was the source of 36 per cent of the world's total exports of vaccines, second only to the European Union (38 per cent) and substantially higher than either the United States (13 per cent), India (2.4 per cent) or Russia (2.1 per cent). When domestically delivered doses are included, China is world's largest producer of COVID-19 vaccines.

The distribution of China's commercial exports of vaccines

This section presents the data on the geographical distribution of commercial sales of Chinese vaccines in the Global South during the initial months of the global vaccine rollout. The data suggest that two key factors shaped these sales: first (as with most international trade), the economic size and population of importing countries; and second, the clinical trial partnerships that Chinese vaccine companies developed with certain countries due to the need to conduct studies on vaccine efficacy overseas.

Figure 4.3 maps deliveries of commercial sales of Chinese COVID-19 vaccine doses in the Global South. As the figure illustrates, countries receiving a large proportion of Chinese vaccines on a commercial basis shared two key features: first, they had large populations; and second, they were middle-income (as opposed to low-income) economies. During the first six months of 2021, China's largest customers by far were Indonesia and Brazil, followed by Mexico, Pakistan and Morocco. This points toward standard 'gravity' explanations for sales of Chinese vaccines. The gravity model, which is widely utilized by economists to explain patterns in international trade, suggests that countries trade more with those that are larger in size (measured by population and GDP) and closer (Head and Mayer, 2014). Put simply, places with lots of people needing protection and with the resources to pay for them bought the most Chinese vaccine doses.

However, a closer examination of which countries were able to purchase vaccines from each manufacturer (and get them delivered) also illustrates the importance of the stage three clinical trial deals between Sinopharm, Sinovac and CanSino and their international partners in ensuring early access. Table 4.1 summarizes the main customers for each manufacturer.[14]

The data suggest that over two thirds of Sinovac's commercial deliveries during the first half of 2021 went to just two countries: Indonesia and Brazil. These are both populous middle-income countries, and were also Sinovac's earliest clinical trial partners. Likewise, over one third of Sinopharm's initial commercial deliveries to the Global South went to Morocco, one of its early trial partners, with another trial partner Peru receiving just under one tenth of them. As discussed further in the concluding chapter of this book, over

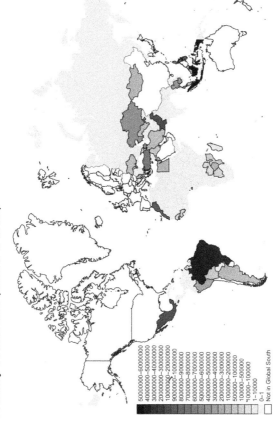

Figure 4.3: Map of delivered sales of Chinese vaccines in the Global South, 1 January–30 June 2021 (number of doses)

Maps compiled using Stata, © Copyright 1996–2022 StataCorp LLC.

Table 4.1: Chinese vaccine sales delivered to the Global South, top countries by manufacturer, 1 January–30 June 2021

Country	% of doses*	Region	Income category	Trial partner in 2020
Sinovac				
Indonesia	33%	Asia	Lower-middle income	Yes
Brazil	31%	Latin America and the Caribbean	Upper-middle income	Yes
Pakistan	6%	Asia	Lower-middle income	No
Mexico	6%	Latin America and the Caribbean	Upper-middle income	No
Philippines	6%	Asia	Lower-middle income	No
Sinopharm				
Morocco	37%	Africa	Lower-middle income	Yes
Pakistan	9%	Asia	Lower-middle income	No
Peru	8%	Latin America and the Caribbean	Upper-middle income	Yes

Table 4.1: Chinese vaccine sales delivered to the Global South, top countries by manufacturer, 1 January–30 June 2021 (continued)

Country	% of doses*	Region	Income category	Trial partner in 2020
Mongolia	7%	Asia	Lower-middle income	No
Indonesia	6%	Asia	Lower-middle income	No
CanSino				
Mexico	98%	Latin America and the Caribbean	Upper-middle income	Yes
Pakistan	1%	Asia	Lower-middle income	Yes

Notes: * refers to the percentage of total delivered commercial supplies of doses from the manufacturer to the Global South during the first six months of 2021. The data do not include doses that are committed but not delivered, doses for which the manufacturer is unclear, or donations.

Source: Compiled by author from own data. Information on clinical trial start dates and locations comes from the COVID-19 vaccine tracker (Basta and Moodie, n.d.), which in turn draws mainly from the US National Library of Medicine's clinical studies registry and results database (https://clinicaltrials.gov/). Income categories are World Bank country lending groups.

the longer term these early clinical trial deals also paved the way for manufacturing cooperation, helping those countries that secured them establish local facilities to make the Chinese vaccines originally developed in Beijing, Tianjin and Wuhan.

It is unclear whether Chinese manufacturers deliberately sought out countries with larger potential markets to conduct clinical trials: the statements from company leaders in the section above suggests they were guided mainly by the practical realities of conducting trials effectively and quickly. However, the features that make a country a good potential customer also tend to make it a good place to conduct trials (high demand due to both population and disease prevalence, as well as healthcare infrastructure).

Africa left behind

As previous chapters detail, while Africa is the traditional locus of Chinese foreign assistance, the Chinese government's early vaccine donations were concentrated not on that continent but instead in China's neighbours. Likewise, as the data in this chapter show, Africa (with a few notable exceptions) was left behind in commercial sales of vaccines from Chinese companies. On the one hand, this is unsurprising. Africa forms a very small proportion of Chinese trade in general, and most African states have less buying power than their (mostly) wealthier counterparts in Asia and Latin America. Less established healthcare infrastructure also made many African countries less practicable destinations for clinical trials by Chinese manufacturers.

On the other hand, China's (lack of) provision of vaccines to Africa magnifies the misguided 'grand strategy of vaccine diplomacy' versus 'global public good' debate. China is viewed by some, mostly in the West, as seeking to dominate Africa, first through 'debt trap diplomacy'[15] (Chellaney, 2017)[16], and more recently through vaccines. Conversely, some, mostly in China, seek to portray the 'global public good' of Chinese vaccines as the solution to the pandemic on the continent. In reality, in the initial global rollout of vaccines, most of Africa was left out of both aid and trade. (However, as the concluding chapter outlines, as the exchange of COVID-19 vaccines increasingly becomes a routine transaction, and as the continent develops its own production capacity in part due to cooperation with China, there are hopeful signs that this situation is changing.) The fact that Africa features so heavily in the narrative on Chinese vaccines in the Global South, and so lightly in the reality of the initial rollout, points to the importance of empirical data and objective, nuanced analysis in understanding both China–Africa relations and China's broader foreign policy and economic behaviour.

Conclusion

The vast majority of Chinese-made vaccines delivered overseas are the result of commercial deals between Chinese manufacturers and their customers, not foreign aid from the Chinese government. Understanding the forces shaping the behaviour of Chinese vaccine companies is therefore crucial to explaining patterns in the country's vaccine supplies to the Global South more broadly.

During the early rollout of vaccinations, Chinese firms (alongside AstraZeneca) were the major source of doses for low- and middle-income states. Unlike AstraZeneca, however, their competitive advantage was accessibility, not affordability. The three major players in the early international rollout of Chinese vaccines – the state owned behemoth Sinopharm, and the two younger, and smaller private players Sinovac and CanSino – were each able to leverage financial and administrative support from the state to develop and commercialize their vaccine candidates extremely quickly.

Moreover, given China's tight pandemic controls at home, the country did not face the same pressures as other industrialized states to take defensive measures such as export bans or large scale advance purchase orders. As a result, for the first half of 2021, Chinese manufacturers were some of the few that were delivering to the Global South. These early sales were shaped by simple economic gravity (population size and wealth), and by the priority access garnered by some states, notably Brazil, Indonesia, Mexico, Morocco and Pakistan, through partnership deals to host clinical trials, which had in turn been necessitated by China's low COVID-19 rates domestically.

FIVE

Conclusion: Between Politics and Business

This concluding chapter summarizes the key arguments of the book, draws broader lessons for students of IPE and China's overseas engagement, and takes a forward facing tentative look at some of the challenges and opportunities facing China and its international partners in the area of COVID-19 vaccines. Challenges include efficacy questions posed by new variants, and increased competition, in particular from vaccines using mRNA technology. Opportunities include the potential for Chinese homegrown development of mRNA vaccines, and (perhaps most importantly of all) prospects for technology transfer and manufacturing partnerships that may reduce the dependence of the Global South on outside sources for this critical commodity.

Key arguments and implications

Chinese vaccine supplies to the Global South have attracted substantial global attention, and sparked a polarized debate. On the one hand, the Chinese government is accused by some, mostly in the West, of using COVID-19 vaccines as a tool of strategic geopolitical competition with the United States and its allies, or as a 'trap' with which to secure policy concessions from governments of smaller countries. On the other hand, China's official discourse frames the country's vaccines as a 'global public good', in other words freely and equally available to all.

This debate was particularly salient during the first half of 2021, when China was one of the few countries willing to deliver (as opposed to simply pledge or commit) vaccine doses overseas, and the media in North America and Europe became preoccupied with the notion that China was 'beating' the West in the race to vaccinate the world (Smith, 2021). However, it remains highly relevant today, given that a significant minority of the world's population lacks access to vaccines (Mathieu et al, 2021), and new variants and booster programmes indicate that COVID-19 vaccination is likely to become a routine feature of life over the long term, rather than a one-off pandemic-ending event.

This book's central contribution is to look beyond the polarized rhetorical debates to examine where doses of Chinese-made vaccines actually went during the 'first wave' of the global rollout vaccines for COVID-19, and to provide empirically grounded, objective, and nuanced explanations for those patterns. In so doing, it hopes to contribute to better understanding of what shapes China's international engagement and its role in the world.

In brief, it has argued that fears of a Chinese grand strategy to reshape global order via so-called 'vaccine diplomacy' are not helpful in explaining the actual distribution of Chinese vaccines. However, the official framing of vaccine supplies as freely and equally available to all is challenged by the practical reality of constrained supplies and the need to make trade-offs, and by the fact that the majority of Chinese-made vaccines shipped overseas were (like most vaccines made in other countries) sold rather than donated.

To understand China's vaccine supplies to the Global South, we need to look inside China, to the 'opportunity management' of state and corporate actors in the context of the pandemic (Jing, 2021; Kuhlmann et al, 2021), which presented both challenges and opportunities. In brief, this had three features. The first was strict and largely effective pandemic control at home during 2020 and 2021. The second was to prioritize nearby countries for vaccine donations, with the objectives of 'moving the anti-pandemic barrier forward' by mitigating imported infections, preserving regional stability, and bolstering established partnerships. These first two features were largely motivated by the party-state's need to maintain performance legitimacy domestically, to which regional stability has long been key, and to which pandemic management has more recently become central. The third feature was to leverage strong state–corporate linkages and pre-existing mechanisms for supporting scientific innovation to become a large and successful player in global vaccine markets. The latter was driven by simple commercial imperatives of the companies involved, and by the Chinese government's longstanding aim of building a more innovative economic model.

As such, during the first half of 2021 Chinese vaccine donations were concentrated in its Asian neighbours (and not in Africa, as is frequently assumed). Meanwhile, commercial exports were weighted toward countries with large populations and the money to pay for them, and to those locations that established clinical trial partnerships with Chinese vaccine manufacturers that enabled them to test their vaccines and so bring their products to market quickly. These were principally (although not exclusively) middle-income emerging economies in Asia and Latin America.

Both business *and* politics are therefore important in understanding the distribution of Chinese vaccines overseas. However, the former is much more important than 'grand strategy' explanations for Chinese vaccine supplies allow for, while the latter is principally rooted in domestic factors, in particular the need of the party-state to maintain performance legitimacy through (the perception of) effective governance, rather than geopolitical competition with the West.

The analysis in this book has implications both for the study of international political economy in general and for the understandings of China's overseas engagement specifically. First, for scholars of IPE, who are usually more accustomed to studying routine aid, trade and other exchanges, the COVID-19 pandemic raised the question of the extent to which crises are catalysts for change or magnifiers of existing structures, patterns and interests. This analysis suggests they are both. On the one hand, China's state and corporate actors seized on the opportunity of the pandemic to turn Chinese vaccine manufacturers from relative obscurity into major global players. On the other, their interests, strategies and actions were shaped by pre-existing conditions. The Chinese government prioritized stability, as it nearly always does. Donations shared many common features with existing Chinese aid. Pre-existing state–corporate linkages aimed at delivering the longstanding goal of an innovation driven economy were reoriented to facilitate the development and marketization of coronavirus vaccines.

Second, for scholars of China's economy and politics, it highlights that vaccine supplies to the Global South – like other aspects of China's globalization – are driven not by a single grand strategy but by a complex set of political and economic interests. However, unlike the 'fragmented authoritarianism' literature, it emphasizes the role of the state as a coordinated and coordinating actor during periods of crisis. It also highlights that Africa – while featuring heavily in rhetoric on China's relations with the Global South, as well as in Chinese diplomacy – was in general not prioritized during the crisis, at least in terms of the distribution of vaccines. This reflects the importance of domestic and commercial imperatives over grand strategy. Most African states were not at the top of the list for Chinese vaccines, with the exceptions of clinical trial hosts in North Africa and a very small selection of longstanding partners.

Nonetheless, there are signs that – as the crisis subsides and the gap between demand and supply of vaccine abates – Chinese vaccine supplies are rebalancing toward Africa. In particular, in November 2021 Chinese President Xi Jinping announced the provision of one billion doses of Chinese vaccines to the continent in 2022, with 600 million donated and 400 million through manufacturing agreements (more on this below) (CGTN, 2021a).

Looking forward: the future of Chinese vaccines in the Global South

Almost every aspect of the short history of the COVID-19 pandemic cautions against making predictions. Nonetheless, this final section of the book explores some longer term developments in China's role in the provision of COVID-19 vaccines around the world, and offers a tentative look at the challenges and opportunities in this area going forward.

Challenges

During the initial months of the global vaccine rollout, the key competitive advantage of Chinese-made vaccines was their accessibility to the Global South. Unlike most other places with the ability to make COVID-19 vaccines, China was delivering at scale, at least in certain regions. However, from around the summer of 2021, the substantial progress made by other vaccine supplying countries in domestic inoculation, as well as increases in production capacity, meant that vaccines from other sources became increasingly available to countries of the Global South (WTO and IMF, n.d.). The United States, which had thus far pledged vaccines for low- and middle-income nations, but shipped few of them, delivered over 80 million donated doses overseas in July 2021 (KFF, 2022). India, the main producer of the AstraZeneca vaccine for the Global South, ended its export ban in November 2021, while the European Union eased its export restrictions the following month (European Commission, 2021).

The loss of accessibility as a competitive advantage over other vaccine sources is compounded by the fact that data suggest that, while they *are* effective in providing protection against COVID-19, the Sinopharm and Sinovac vaccines (which are made using inactivated vaccine technology, in which the virus is essentially grown, killed and injected into recipients), are *less* effective than vaccines using newer technologies, in particular mRNA, which transfers instructions on how to make antibodies to cells (Mallapaty, 2021). As such, when other vaccines became available, some countries started to turn to other manufacturers.

The case of Brazil, initially one of Sinovac's largest customers, exemplifies these challenges. Brazil experimented with giving booster shots of other vaccines including Pfizer, Janssen and AstraZeneca to those who had been vaccinated with Sinovac (Costa Clemens et al, 2022), and the country's federal government suspended discussions with the company about buying more doses in September 2021. Former Brazilian health officials told the media that Sinovac's vaccine 'played its role … helped a lot' in the initial rollout but that it was no longer the preferred choice for the country now that other vaccines were accessible (Magalhaes and Pearson, 2021).

Brazil's decision to turn to other vaccine sources was in part sparked by concerns about the then-dominant Delta variant's implications for vaccine efficacy. Data suggest that the Omicron variant further compounds these challenges (Dolgin, 2022), with some studies finding that Sinovac, the most widely used Chinese vaccine, does not provide sufficient protection against Omicron (Hong, 2021), although others indicate that with a booster the vaccine offers good protection against hospitalization and death (Mueller, 2022). Indeed, whether or not new variants reduce the effectiveness of the Chinese vaccines currently on the market so much so that they are significantly less useful weapons against COVID-19, the rhetoric around their effectiveness, and the perception among populations of recipient states that they are less likely to provide protection, may reduce demand in future (Da Fonseca et al, 2021).

Chinese officials and vaccine makers are alert to these challenges (not least because of the need to develop vaccines that can also effectively protect residents in China). As early as March 2021, Wang Juanzhi, deputy head of an expert task force on vaccine development and an academic at the Chinese Academy of Engineering, told the State Council's inter-agency task force briefing on promoting COVID-19 vaccination that new variants were 'an issue of great concern', and that China was taking 'proactive measures to develop a new generation of vaccines' (State Council Information Office, 2021b). As the following section outlines, both established and new players in China have started to explore newer and alternative technologies for making COVID-19 vaccines going forward.

Opportunities

A Chinese mRNA vaccine?

As detailed in Chapter Four, COVID-19 represented an opportunity for Chinese vaccine manufacturers to put themselves on the global map. While doses made by Sinovac and Sinopharm using inactivated vaccine technology dominated China's initial rollout of vaccines internationally and domestically, there are multiple different vaccines using alternative technologies under development by Chinese companies.

Progress on vaccines that use the highly effective mRNA approach utilized by Pfizer and Moderna is proceeding, and includes both some of the companies involved in the initial rollout of Chinese vaccines and new players. The state owned giant Sinopharm is working on its own mRNA vaccine candidate (Riordan and Langley, 2021). CanSino's mRNA vaccine candidate was approved for clinical trials in early April 2022 (Reuters, 2022). However, the furthest ahead Chinese mRNA vaccine candidate (in clinical trials at the time of writing) is being developed by a partnership between two newer entrants to the COVID-19 vaccine market: the private biotech companies, Walvax and Suzhou Abogen, in collaboration with the Chinese Academy of Military Medical Sciences (CAMMS).

Located in Yunnan University Science Park in a high tech development zone and listed on the Shenzhen stock exchange,

Walvax focuses exclusively on vaccines and has seven (non-COVID-19 related) products on the market (Walvax, n.d.). Its partner Suzhou Abogen was founded in 2019 by a former Moderna scientist and specializes in mRNA-based medical products (Suzhou Abogen, n.d.). The partnership's first international phase 3 clinical trials took place in Indonesia and Mexico, countries that also partnered with Sinovac and CanSino respectively for trials (Basta and Moodie, n.d.). Both Walvax and Suzhou Abogen have raised substantial amounts of investment (Chen, 2022), and if their new vaccine is successfully brought to market, these previously relatively unknown firms may – like Sinovac – rise to become prominent players in the global pharmaceutical industry.

However, it is unclear whether the Walvax/Suzhou Abogen mRNA vaccine will live up to these expectations. On the one hand, a crucial advantage of this mRNA candidate compared to others is that it can be stored in a regular refrigerator (in contrast, the Pfizer and Moderna alternatives need to be stored at extremely cold temperatures well below standard refrigeration and therefore are technologically and climatically prohibitive for many Global South countries) (Crommelin et al, 2021; Zhang, 2022). On the other hand, Walvax/Suzhou Abogen face two major challenges. First, some initial data suggests limited effectiveness against the Omicron variant (Watanabe, 2022), although at the time of writing clinical trials have not concluded. Second, the CAMMS, which is partnering with the two firms, is on the United States' 'Entity List' (the same trade restriction list as Chinese tech giant Huawei), which may limit the vaccine's ability to make inroads internationally even if it succeeds in being brought to market within China.

Local manufacturing collaborations

A more definitively promising medium- and long-term consequence of China's role in the provision of vaccinations in the Global South is the establishment of technology transfer and manufacturing deals between Chinese vaccine companies and partners across the Global South. As mentioned in Chapter One, one of the main reasons for the vast and ongoing global inequalities in access to COVID-19 vaccines is the dependence of most low- and middle-income countries on vaccines produced overseas. Africa, for example, still imported 99 per cent of its (non–COVID-19 related) vaccines as of July 2021 (Nkengasong, 2021). Reducing this reliance could be an important step toward more equitable vaccine distribution.

Chinese companies are playing an important and constructive role in this. In many cases, the clinical trial deals made between Sinopharm, Sinovac and CanSino and their international partners ensured not only priority access to doses, but also agreements for those vaccines to be manufactured in the host country once developed. As mentioned in Chapter Three, Pakistan has launched 'PakVac', a homemade COVID-19 vaccine using technology from CanSino, whose clinical trial it hosted (Shahzad, 2021). Likewise, Indonesia's agreement with Sinovac included provisions to supply Biofarma, the country's largest vaccine maker, with the capacity to assemble hundreds of millions of doses per year of the vaccine itself. The country plans to use the deal to become a regional hub for vaccine supply (Sarmiento, 2021). Brazil's Butantan Institute, which partnered with Sinovac to carry out clinical trials, also secured capacity to produce doses locally at scale (Hu and Huang, 2021). Morocco, which hosted Sinopharm trials and landed a manufacturing deal with the company, built capacity to produce more than 3 million doses of the Sinopharm vaccine per month by the end of 2021 (France24, 2022).

As well as reducing dependency on foreign imports and bringing more equitable vaccine distribution, such manufacturing collaborations could be a means of creating economic opportunities in an emerging industry for Global South countries. It appears that COVID-19 will become endemic, and the need for vaccinations against it ongoing. As well as the direct benefits in terms of job creation in vaccine manufacturing facilities, those countries which develop local vaccine making capacity through international collaborations are likely to benefit from technology and knowledge spillovers, with benefits for the broader pharmaceutical sector and other industries.

Closing thoughts

This book takes a look beyond the polarized rhetoric to explore the where, how and why, of the initial rollout of Chinese vaccines to the Global South. It aims to leave readers with three key reflections. First, Chinese supplies of COVID-19 vaccines are neither a geopolitical strategy to 'remake world order' nor an altruistic free-for-all: they are driven by a complex set of imperatives, which are rooted much more in domestic commercial and political realities than grand strategy. Second, given that COVID-19 appears here to stay, and China has established itself as a source of vaccinations that protect against it, there are substantial benefits to be had for those in both the Global South and Global North who have a better understanding of China's role in global vaccine aid and trade. Third, the disconnect between the narratives on, and the reality of, China's COVID-19 vaccine supplies to the Global South is representative of a broader need for a more empirically based, objective and nuanced approach to China and its role in the world, particularly among the mass media and policymakers in North America and Europe.

Notes

one   Introduction

[1]   The term 'Global South' is typically used to refer to less economically developed regions including Africa, Asia, Latin America, and Oceania, and to underscore unequal geoeconomic and geopolitical relations of power (Dados and Connell, 2012). While recognizing that the conceptualization and definition of the Global South is contested (Levander and Mignolo, 2011), in this book the Global South is defined as low-, lower middle-, and upper middle-income states as per the World Bank's Country Lending Groups. Low-income economies are those with a Gross National Income (GNI) per capita of US$1045 or less, with the range for lower-middle income economies being US$1046–4095, and for upper middle-income economies US$4096–12,695.

[2]   'Soft power' refers to a nation's power to attract and influence (as opposed to 'hard' military or economic power) (Nye, 1990, 2004).

[3]   The US, European Union and India, for example, all introduced some degree of export controls (Ibrahim, 2021).

[4]   According to the author's data. Other sources of information on Chinese vaccine supplies, including Beijing Bridge's 'China COVID-19 Vaccine Tracker' (n.d.) and Duke University's 'Launch and Scale Speedometer' (n.d.) have similar estimates.

[5]   By the end of 2021, the United States and European Union had become the largest sources of *donated* vaccines, followed by China.

[6]   Of course, increases in production capacity mean the supply of COVID-19 vaccines will eventually become a routine rather than crisis-based exchange. Nonetheless, understanding the factors driving China's initial distribution of vaccines is important contextual knowledge.

[7]   See also Mertha (2005) and Landry (2008) for discussions of the role of subnational actors in Chinese policymaking and implementation.

[8]   In brief, the term 'party-state' refers to the close intertwinement of the Communist Party and the government in China. For an overview of the concept, see Guo (2001). For linguistic convenience, the terms 'party-state', 'state' and 'government' are used interchangeably in this book.

[9]   The author's data indicate that during the first six months of 2021, around 10 per cent of doses were bilateral donations, with 87 per cent sold commercially, and the remaining three per cent unclear. Beijing Bridge's Chinese vaccine tracker, which aggregates Chinese vaccines sold and donated so far, indicates that at the time of writing these proportions remain approximately the same (Beijing Bridge, n.d.).

[10] These data can be found on the website of China's National Bureau of Statistics: https://data.stats.gov.cn/english/.

[11] As is discussed further in Chapter Five, as production capacity expands and supply is less constrained, donations from China have since rebalanced somewhat toward Africa. In particular, President Xi pledged donations of 600 million doses to the continent at the 2021 Forum on China–Africa Cooperation (FOCAC) in November 2021.

[12] In the interests of concision, the full data collection methodology is not described here. However, both the detailed methodology and the data itself are available from the author on request.

[13] When a batch of Chinese vaccines arrives in a partner country, one or all of these organizations typically issue a public report promoting it, accompanied by images of the vaccines' arrival. Likewise, when an agreement is signed for provision of vaccine doses, these organizations often report it, particularly in the case of donations.

[14] However, these were often limited in content and availability.

[15] This was often extremely helpful in filling in gaps in official accounts (for example, Chinese official reports often specified that a certain number doses had been delivered, but not whether they were donated or supplied on a commercial basis, or which company they had been manufactured by).

[16] Given the extremely constrained supply during the period in question, it is important to distinguish between commitments and deliveries, as recipient countries may wait months for announced commitments (both from China and other provider) to be delivered. For vaccine donations, information on commitments versus doses actually shipped by provider country can be found at Duke University's Launch and Scale Speedometer (Duke Global Health Innovation Center, n.d.).

[17] This dataset also includes some information on COVID-19 doses administered by manufacturer, but only for a small, select group of countries which report this information publicly, the vast majority of which are in the Global North. At the time of writing, only two countries of the Global South (Ecuador and Ukraine) are included.

[18] However, the deliveries data are not disaggregated by supplier country or manufacturer, making it impossible to separate Chinese deliveries from other sources.

[19] Importantly, this includes disaggregated information over time and by manufacturer and/or provider country. However, for purchased vaccines (the vast majority) it does not include information on whether a committed consignment of doses was actually delivered and/ or administered.

[20] This includes a breakdown of how many of these doses are provided as bilateral donations, alongside COVAX. However, purchased vaccine

supplies are not disaggregated by source country or manufacturer, and the data are not disaggregated by date.

[21] This includes information on vaccines purchased and/or donation, and doses actually delivered, and aggregated information on doses per Chinese manufacturing company. However, this information is not disaggregated by date, precluding analysis of changes over time and of the earlier months of the global vaccine rollout.

[22] Our World in Data collates official data on vaccines administered by manufacturer over time for those countries which publish it; however, these are almost all in the Global North.

two   Contextualizing China's Position in Global Health

[1] These data can be found via the World Bank's World Development Indicators: https://data.worldbank.org/indicator/SP.DYN.LE00. IN?locations=CN-US.

[2] For a detailed overview of China's domestic healthcare system, see Burns and Liu (2017).

[3] The 'Hu-Wen' era refers to the leadership of President Hu Jintao and Premier Wen Jiabao, who directly preceded Xi Jinping.

[4] The WHO is funded by member states, who are required to make assessed contributions and may make voluntary contributions if they wish, as well as other international organizations, philanthropic entities and the private sector.

[5] Prequalification is a WHO evaluation process that serves as an indicator to UN agencies which procure vaccines that a given vaccine meets safety, quality and efficacy standards.

three   'Vaccine Diplomacy'

[1] For example, in announcing a plan to donate 80 million doses in May 2021, US President Joe Biden stated 'You know, there's a lot of talk about Russia and China influencing the world with vaccines. We want to lead the world with our values – with this demonstration of our innovation, ingenuity, and the fundamental decency of the American people' (Whitehouse.gov, 2021). Likewise, a USAID (2021) press release commemorates the delivery of 200 million US donations of COVID-19 vaccine doses, pointing to '200 million reasons to be proud'.

[2] US vaccine aid, for example, has been concentrated in Africa (KFF, 2022), while the UK's top vaccine aid recipients are in Africa and Asia (Pockock, 2021).

[3] Another example comes from Xi'an, a major city and capital of Shaanxi province, where several local officials were removed from their posts in January 2022 after failing to control a local outbreak.

[4] The term 'imported infections' should not be taken to imply that people of any particular nationality or origin are more likely to carry the virus. As the data from Zhang et al (2020) suggest, the majority of people testing positive for COVID-19 after entering China are Chinese nationals returning from overseas, which reflects their greater representation among those able to secure entry to China.

[5] 'Top recipients' are defined as those receiving deliveries of 0.5 million or more officially donated vaccine doses from China during the period in question.

[6] These patterns are also corroborated by other sources of data on Chinese vaccine supplies such as Duke's Launch and Scale Speedmeter (Taylor, 2021).

[7] The author's data suggest that approximately 1.4 million doses were donated by the People's Liberation Army, mainly to countries with established close military connections to China, such as Pakistan.

[8] China pledged US$100 million in funding for COVAX in August 2021 – Beijing's biggest voluntary donation to an international organization to date – potentially signaling a greater willingness to contribute on a multilateral rather than bilateral basis going forward (GAVI, n.d.).

[9] For the remainder the manufacturer is unknown.

[10] As a result of their absence from any Chinese official sources, the donations to the rebels are not included in the author's quantitative data on Chinese vaccine supplies. Nonetheless, given the number of media reports from reliable organizations detailing their existence, they are included in this case study as evidence of the critical imperative of the Chinese government to control the risk of imported infections.

[11] Tashkurgan, the town closest to the border on the Chinese side, is over 100 kilometres away from the main crossing point between the two countries.

[12] Pakistan was one of the first countries to be allowed to resume direct flights to Beijing in September 2020 after all international flights to the capital were re-routed to other destinations from March 2020 to minimize the risk of sparking an outbreak in the China's capital city (*Global Times*, 2020).

[13] Li and Ye (2019) classify the China–Nepal relationship as level 3 / a 'regular partnership', the China–Philippines relationship is level 2 / a 'strategic partnership', and China–Zimbabwe as lacking a formal partnership. After their research was conducted, the China–Nepal relationship was upgraded to a 'strategic partnership of cooperation' / level 2 (CGTN, 2019), the China–Philippines relationship was upgraded to a 'comprehensive strategic partnership' / level 1 (Ministry of Foreign Affairs

of the People's Republic of China, 2021), and China and Zimbabwe established a 'comprehensive strategic partnership' (Ministry of Foreign Affairs of the People's Republic of China, 2018).

[14] As of as of 3 January 2022.

[15] The author's data set records official donations of Chinese vaccines in February and May of 2021, but the amounts are unknown.

four   Market Forces and Commercial Chinese Vaccine Sales

[1] For an exception see a report on the topic by the Center for Strategic and International Studies (CSIS, 2021).

[2] Duke University's Launch and Scale Speedometer (n.d.) data likewise indicate that as of the end of 2021 87 per cent of Chinese vaccine doses committed abroad were commercial sales, while 13 per cent were donations. Beijing Bridge's (n.d.) tracker confirms this trend: as of January 2022, it counted 92 per cent of Chinese vaccine commitments as commercial sales, and 8 per cent as donations.

[3] These statistics are calculated from Duke University's Global Health Innovation Center Launch and Scale Speedometer archive, 2 July 2021 update.

[4] The remainder involved global entities such as COVAX.

[5] These statistics are calculated from Duke University's Global Health Innovation Center Center Launch and Scale Speedometer archive, 2 July 2021 update.

[6] Data on vaccine deliveries over time disaggregated across all global manufacturers is not publicly available at the time of writing.

[7] See Callaway (2020) for a more detailed account of how wealthy nations bought up vaccine stocks through pre-orders. Also see Wouters et. al. (2021) for a study of challenges in global access to COVID-19 vaccines, which similarly rates the Sinopharm and Sinovac vaccines highly in terms of accessibility but low in terms of affordability.

[8] The profit seeking behaviour of pharmaceutical firms during the pandemic has been widely critiqued. This book is an empirical, rather than normative, study, and a discussion of the ethics of such behaviour are therefore beyond its scope. For an ethical argument against profit-seeking from the distribution of COVID-19 vaccines, see Binagwaho et al (2021).

[9] One of these, Sinopharm, has approved vaccines developed by two different subsidiaries, Sinopharm (Beijing) and Sinopharm (Wuhan).

[10] The description of CNBG's history in this paragraph is summarized from the company's website (CNBG, 2021).

[11] Vaccines go through three standard stages of human trials: first, small-scale trials to evaluate safety; second, small-scale trials to evaluate safety and efficacy; and third, trials involving many participants, also to evaluate safety and efficacy across large groups of people.

[12] In Sinopharm's case this also included high income countries such as the United Arab Emirates and Bahrain. Sinopharm's engagement with these countries is beyond the scope of this book.

[13] China is far from alone in having a military that is engaged in medical research. The US military has been involved in research into vaccines against diseases such as HIV for decades (Reilly, 2010; Ratto-Kim et al., 2018), and more recently aims to develop a 'universal' vaccine against COVID-19 (Thompson, 2021).

[14] This includes the top five customers for Sinovac and Sinopharm, and the only two customers to actually receive commercial shipments from CanSino during this period.

[15] For excellent academic analyses that explain why so-called 'debt trap diplomacy' is a myth, see Brautigam (2020), or Singh (2021).

[16] Chellaney's (2017) original article on 'debt-trap diplomacy' focuses on South and Southeast Asia. However, the term has since become used to describe China's relations with the wider Global South, in particular with Africa.

References

Adlakha, H. (2020) 'Did China join COVAX to counter or promote vaccine nationalism?', *The Diplomat*, [online] 23 October. Available from: https://thediplomat.com/2020/10/did-china-join-covax-to-counter-or-promote-vaccine-nationalism/

Ahmar, M. (2020) 'Dynamics of Pakistan-China relations', *Journal of Security and Strategic Analyses*, 6(1): 86–106.

Akhtar, H., Afridi, M., Akhtar, A., Ahmad, H., Ali, S., Khalid, S., Awan, S.M., Jahangiri, S. and Khader, Y.S. (2021) 'Pakistan's response to COVID-19: overcoming national and international hypes to fight the pandemic', *JMIR Public Health and Surveillance*, 7(5): doi: 10.2196/28517.

Anoko, J.N., Barry, B.R., Boiro, H., Diallo, B., Diallo, A.B., Belizaire, M.R., Keita, M., Djingarey, M.H., N'da, M.Y., Yoti, Z., Fall, I.-S. and Talisuna, A. (2020) 'Community engagement for successful COVID-19 pandemic response: 10 lessons from Ebola outbreak responses in Africa', *BMJ Global Health*, 4(Suppl 7): doi: 10.1136/bmjgh-2020-003121.

ASEAN Post (2021) 'Myanmar rebels get COVID jabs from China', [online] 25 July. Available from: https://theaseanpost.com/article/myanmar-rebels-get-covid-jabs-china

Asundi, A., O'Leary, C. and Bhadelia, N. (2021) 'Global COVID-19 vaccine inequity: The scope, the impact, and the challenges', *Cell Host & Microbe*, 29(7): 1036–39.

Basta, N. and Moodie, E. (n.d.) 'COVID-19 vaccine development and approvals tracker', [online] VIPER (Vaccines, Infectious disease Prevention, and Epidemiology Research) Group. Available from: https://covid19.trackvaccines.org/

Bate, R. and Porter, K. (2009) 'The problems and potential of China's pharmaceutical industry', *AEI Health Policy Outlook*, [online] 23 April. Available from: www.aei.org/research-products/report/the-problems-and-potential-of-chinas-pharmaceutical-industry/

BBC News (2021) 'Coronavirus: EU sues AstraZeneca over vaccine delivery delays', [online] 26 April. Available from: www.bbc.com/news/world-europe-56891326

BBC News (2022) 'China: Xi'an residents in lockdown trade goods for food amid shortage', [online] 4 January. Available from: www.bbc.com/news/world-asia-china-59864266

Beaumont, P. (2021) 'Delhi reportedly halts AstraZeneca Covid vaccine exports as cases soar', *The Guardian*, [online] 24 March. Available from: www.theguardian.com/world/2021/mar/24/delhi-reportedly-halts-astrazeneca-covid-vaccine-exports-as-cases-soar

Beijing Bridge (n.d.) 'China COVID-19 Vaccine Tracker' [online]. Available from: https://bridgebeijing.com/our-publications/our-publications-1/china-covid-19-vaccines-tracker/#Methodology

Binagwaho, A., Mathewos, K. and Davis, S. (2021) 'Time for the ethical management of COVID-19 vaccines', *The Lancet Global Health*, 9(8): doi: 10.1016/S2214-109X(21)00180-7.

Bloomberg (2021) 'Covid shot lifts China's CanSino to profitability for first time', [online] 28 August. Available from: www.bloomberg.com/news/articles/2021-08-28/covid-shot-lifts-china-s-cansino-to-profitability-for-first-time

Boettke, P. and Powell, B. (2021) 'The political economy of the COVID-19 pandemic', *Southern Economic Journal*, 87: 1090–106.

Bouey, J. (2020) 'Strengthening China's public health response system: from SARS to COVID-19', *American Journal of Public Health*, 110(7): 939–40.

Brautigam, D. (2020) 'A critical look at Chinese "debt-trap diplomacy": the rise of a meme', *Area Development and Policy*, 5(1): 1–14.

Breslin, S. (2013) 'China and the South: objectives, actors and interactions', *Development and Change*, 44(6): 1273–94.

Brødsgaard, K.E. (2017) *Chinese Politics as Fragmented Authoritarianism*, New York: Routledge.

Burke, J., Wintour, P. and Ratcliffe, R. (2021) 'Covid vaccines: India export delay deals blow to poorer countries', *The Guardian*, [online] 19 May. Available from: www.theguardian.com/world/2021/may/19/poorer-countries-face-long-delays-receiving-covid-vaccines

Burki, T. (2020) 'Global shortage of personal protective equipment', *The Lancet. Infectious Diseases*, 20(7): 785–86.

Burns, L.R. and Liu, G.G. (eds) (2017) *China's Healthcare System and Reform*, Cambridge: Cambridge University Press.

Businesswire (2020) 'Sinovac reports unaudited fourth quarter 2019 financial results and files 2019 annual report on Form 20-F', [online] 30 April. Available from: www.businesswire.com/news/home/20200430005994/en/Sinovac-Reports-Unaudited-Fourth-Quarter-2019-Financial-Results-and-Files-2019-Annual-Report-on-Form-20-F

Callaway, E. (2020) 'The unequal scramble for coronavirus vaccines – by the numbers', *Nature News Explainer*, [online] 24 August. Available from: www.nature.com/articles/d41586-020-02450-x

Campbell, C. (2020) '"We will share our vaccine with the world.": inside the Chinese biotech firm leading the fight against COVID-19', *Time*, [online] 27 July. Available from: https://time.com/5872081/sinovac-covid19-coronavirus-vaccine-coronavac/

CanSino (2021) 'CanSinoBio's COVID-19 vaccine phase III production base has started production, helping to speed up the construction of an immunity barrier', [in Chinese, online] 26 April. Available from: www.cansinotech.com.cn/html/1///179/180/966.html

Censolo, R. and Morelli, M. (2020) 'COVID-19 and the potential consequences for social stability', *Peace Economics, Peace Science and Public Policy*, 26(3): 1–5.

CEPI (2021) 'COVAX: CEPI's response to COVID-19'. Available from: https://cepi.net/covax/

CGTN (2019) 'China, Nepal agree to lift ties to new height', [online] 13 October. Available from: news.cgtn.com/news/2019-10-12/China-Nepal-agree-to-lift-ties-to-new-height-KJPk5S8VWg/index.html

CGTN (2020) 'Dialogue with Yu Xuefeng: COVID-19 vaccine development', [online] 3 September. Available from: www.youtube.com/watch?v=lCPX48eqB9E

CGTN (2021a) 'China-Africa friendship continues to flourish on vaccine, trade, renewable energy', [online] 30 November. Available from: https://news.cgtn.com/news/2021-11-29/Xi-addresses-opening-ceremony-of-8th-FOCAC-ministerial-conference-15At0m8AIOk/index.html

CGTN (2021b) 'China donates COVID-19 vaccines to 80 countries, 3 intl organizations', [online] 30 March. Available from: https://news.cgtn.com/news/2021-03-30/China-donates-COVID-19-vaccines-to-80-countries-3-intl-organizations-Z3qXfK0jNm/index.html

CGTN (2021c) 'Indonesian President receives Chinese vaccine as rollout begins', [online] 13 January. Available from: www.youtube.com/watch?v=Sf-yLxNbanw

Cha, S. and Kim, M. (2020) '"At war time speed", China leads COVID-19 vaccine race', Reuters, [online] 7 July. Available from: https://www.reuters.com/article/us-health-coronavirus-china-vaccine-anal/at-war-time-speed-china-leads-covid-19-vaccine-race-idUSKBN2481NO

Chan, L.-H. (2011) China Engages Global Health Governance: Responsible Stakeholder or System-Transformer? New York: Palgrave Macmillan.

Chan, L.-H., Chen, L. and Xu, J. (2012) 'China's engagement with global health diplomacy: was SARS a watershed?', PLOS Med, 7(4), https://doi.org/10.1371/journal.pmed.1000266

Chan, L.H., Lee, P.K. and Chan, G. (2009) 'China engages global health governance: processes and dilemmas', Global Public Health, 4(1): 1–30.

Chellaney, B. (2017) 'China's debt-trap diplomacy', Project Syndicate, [online] 23 January. Available from: www.project-syndicate.org/commentary/china-one-belt-one-road-loans-debt-by-brahma-chellaney-2017-01

Chen, Y. (2022) 'Finding China's Moderna is a financial long shot', Reuters, [online] 6 January. Available from: www.reuters.com/breakingviews/finding-chinas-moderna-is-financial-long-shot-2022-01-06/

Chick, H. (2021) 'Coronavirus: border city chief dismissed for Covid-19 failures as Ruili continues to report new cases', *South China Morning Post*, [online] 8 April. Available from: www.scmp.com/news/china/politics/article/3128727/coronavirus-border-city-chief-dismissed-covid-19-failures-ruili

China Daily (2021) 'Chinese vaccines help global COVID-19 fight', [online] 27 October. Available from: www.chinadaily.com.cn/a/202110/27/WS6178a74aa310cdd39bc71834.html

China International Development Cooperation Agency (2021) '500000 doses of Chinese-aided COVID-19 vaccinations provided to Myanmar are delivered to Yangon', [in Chinese, online] 6 May. Available from: www.cidca.gov.cn/2021-05/06/c_1211143857.htm

CNBG (2021) 'Development path' [in Chinese, online]. Available from: www.cnbg.com.cn/#/aboutUs/developHistory?cid=16

Cohen, J. (2020) 'China's vaccine gambit', Science, [online] 25 November. Available from: www.science.org/content/article/global-push-covid-19-vaccines-china-aims-win-friends-and-cut-deals

Costa Clemens, S.A., Weckx, L., Clemens, R., Alemeida Mendes, A.V., Ramos Souza, A., Silveira, M. et al (2022) 'Heterologous versus homologous COVID-19 booster vaccination in previous recipients of two doses of CoronaVac COVID-19 vaccine in Brazil (RHH-001): a phase 4, non-inferiority, single blind, randomised study', *The Lancet*, 399(10324): doi: 10.1016/S0140-6736(22)00094-0.

Cotula, L. (2021) 'Towards a political economy of the COVID-19 crisis: Reflections on an agenda for research and action', *World Development*, 138: doi: 10.1016/j.worlddev.2020.105235.

Croft, A. (2021) 'Russia has an unlikely new social media star: Its Sputnik COVID vaccine', *Fortune*, [online] 24 March. Available from: https://fortune.com/2021/03/24/russia-sputnik-covid-vaccine-social-media-star/

Crommelin, D.J.A., Anchordoquy, T.J., Volkin, D.B., Jiskoot, W. and Mastrobattista, E. (2021) 'Addressing the cold reality of mRNA vaccine stability', *Journal of Pharmaceutical Sciences*, 110(3): 997–1001.

CSIS (2021) 'Is China's Covid-19 diplomacy succeeding?' [online] 23 September. Available from: https://chinapower.csis.org/china-covid-medical-vaccine-diplomacy/

Cull, N.J. (2021) 'From soft power to reputational security: rethinking public diplomacy and cultural diplomacy for a dangerous age', *Place Branding and Public Diplomacy*, 18: doi: 10.1057/s41254-021-00236-0.

Custer, S., Dreher, A., Elston, T.-B., Fuchs, A., Ghose, S., Lin, J.J. et al (2021) 'Tracking Chinese development finance: an application of AidData's TUFF 2.0 methodology', *AidData*, [online] 29 September. Available from: www.aiddata.org/publi cations/aiddata-tuff-methodology-version-2-0

Da Fonseca, E.M., Shadlen, K.C. and Bastos, F.I. (2021) 'The politics of COVID-19 vaccination in middle-income countries: lessons from Brazil', Social *Science & Medicine*, 281, https://doi.org/10.1016/j.socscimed.2021.114 093

Dados, N. and Connell, R. (2012) 'The Global South', *Contexts*, 11(1): 12–13.

Deng, S.-Q. and Peng, H.-J. (2020) 'Characteristics of and public health responses to the coronavirus disease 2019 outbreak in China', *Journal of Clinical Medicine*, 9(2): doi: 10.3390/jcm9020575.

Dolgin, E. (2022) 'Omicron thwarts some of the world's most-used COVID vaccines', *Nature News*, [online] 13 January. Available from: www.nature.com/articles/d41586-022-00079-6

Douglas, R.G. and Samant, V.B. (2018) 'The vaccine industry', Plotkin's Vaccines, 41-50.e1: doi: 10.1016/B978-0-323-35761-6.00004-3.

Dreher, A., Fuchs, A., Parks, B., Strange, A. and Tierney, M.J. (2022) *Banking on Beijing: The Aims and Impacts of China's Overseas Development Program*, Cambridge: Cambridge University Press.

Duke Global Health Innovation Center (n.d.) 'Launch and scale speedometer'. Available from: https://launchandscalefaster.org/covid-19

Eaton, L. (2021) 'Covid-19: WHO warns against "vaccine nationalism" or face further virus mutations', *BMJ*, 372: doi: 10.1136/bmj.n292.

El Azami, H. (2021) 'The large-scale vaccination campaign against COVID-19 in Morocco relies heavily on Chinese vaccine, Beijing Review, [online] 1 March. Available from: www.bjreview.com/World/202103/t20210303_800238119.html

Ellis, S. (2018) 'China's trillion-dollar plan to dominate global trade', *Vox*, [online] 6 April. Available from: www.vox.com/2018/4/6/17206230/china-trade-belt-road-economy

European Commission (2021) 'EU replaces COVID-19 vaccines export authorisation mechanism with new monitoring tool', [online] 26 November. Available from: https://ec.europa.eu/commission/presscorner/detail/en/ip_21_6283

Fan, H.-J., Gao, H.-W., Ding, H., Zhang, B.-K. and Hou, S.-K. (2015) 'The Ebola threat: China's response to the West African epidemic and national development of prevention and control policies and infrastructure', *Disaster Medicine and Public Health Preparedness*, 9(1): 64–5.

Fang, S. and Stone, R. W. (2012) 'International organizations as policy advisors', *International Organization*, 66(4): 537–69.

Farhadi, N. and Lahooti, H. (2021) 'Are COVID-19 data reliable? A quantitative analysis of pandemic data from 182 countries', *COVID*, 1(1): doi: 10.3390/covid1010013.

Feldwisch-Drentrup, H. (2020) 'How WHO Became China's Coronavirus Accomplice', *Foreign Policy*, [online] 20 April. Available from: https://foreignpolicy.com/2020/04/02/china-coronavirus-who-health-soft-power/

Feng, E. (2021) 'One Chinese town has started a fiery online debate about China's zero-COVID policy', *NPR*, [online] 5 November. Available from: www.npr.org/sections/goatsandsoda/2021/11/05/1052811962/one-chinese-town-has-started-a-fiery-online-debate-about-chinas-zero-covid-polic

Fortune (2022) 'Global 500: Sinopharm'. Available from: https://fortune.com/company/sinopharm/global500/

France24 (2021) 'Shots in the dark: China sends Covid aid to Myanmar rebels', [online] 22 September. Available from: www.france24.com/en/live-news/20210922-shots-in-the-dark-china-sends-covid-aid-to-myanmar-rebels

France24 (2022) 'Morocco starts construction of anti-Covid vaccine plant', [online] 27 January. Available from: www.france24.com/en/live-news/20220127-morocco-starts-construction-of-anti-covid-vaccine-plant

Frankel Pratt, S. and Levin, J. (2021) 'Vaccines will shape the new geopolitical order', *Foreign Policy*, [online] 29 April. Available from: https://foreignpolicy.com/2021/04/29/vaccine-geopolitics-diplomacy-israel-russia-china/

Freeman, C. (2011) 'Fragile edges between security and insecurity: China's border regions', in R. Guo and C. Freeman (eds) *Managing Fragile Regions: Method and Application*, New York: Springer, pp 23–46.

Ganesan, N. (2011) 'Myanmar–China relations: interlocking interests but independent output', *Japanese Journal of Political Science*, 12(1): 95–111.

Gao, Q., Bao, L., Mao, H., Wang, L., Xu, K., Yang, M. et al (2020) 'Rapid development of an inactivated vaccine for SARS-CoV-2', *bioRxiv*, [online] 19 April, Available from: www.biorxiv.org/content/10.1101/2020.04.17.046375v1

Garlick, J. (2018) 'Deconstructing the China–Pakistan economic corridor: pipe dreams versus geopolitical realities', *Journal of Contemporary China*, 27(112): 519–33.

Garrison, C. (2020) 'How the "Oxford" Covid-19 vaccine became the "AstraZeneca" Covid-19 vaccine', *Medicines Law & Policy*, [online] 5 October. Available from: https://medicineslawandpolicy.org/2020/10/how-the-oxford-covid-19-vaccine-became-the-astrazeneca-covid-19-vaccine/

GAVI (n.d.) 'Donor profile: China'. Available from: www.gavi.org/investing-gavi/funding/donor-profiles/china

Ghiselli, A. (2021) *Protecting China's Interests Overseas: Securitization and Foreign Policy*, Oxford: Oxford University Press.

Gill, I. and Schellekens, P. (2021) 'COVID-19 is a developing country pandemic', *Brookings*, [online] 27 May. Available from: www.brookings.edu/blog/future-development/2021/05/27/covid-19-is-a-developing-country-pandemic/

Global Times (2020) 'Beijing will resume direct international flights on Thursday', [online] 2 September. Available from: www.globaltimes.cn/content/1199666.shtml

Greenwald, M.B. and Margolis, M.A. (2020) 'Can vaccine diplomacy shape a new world order?', Belfer Center for Science and International Affairs, Harvard Kennedy School, [online] 2 December. Available from: www.belfercenter.org/publication/can-vaccine-diplomacy-shape-new-world-order

Greeven, M. (2020) 'Inside the Chinese companies vying to produce the world's first coronavirus vaccine', *The Conversation*, [online] 27 August. Available from: https://theconversation.com/inside-the-chinese-companies-vying-to-produce-the-worlds-first-coronavirus-vaccine-145146

Guang, L., Roberts, M., Xu, Y. and Zhao, J. (2021) 'Pandemic sees increase in Chinese support for regime, decrease in views towards the U.S.', *UCSD China Data Lab*, [online]. Available from: http://chinadatalab.ucsd.edu/viz-blog/pandemic-sees-increase-in-chinese-support-for-regime-decrease-in-views-towards-us/

Guo, S. (2001) 'The party–state relationship in Post-Mao China', *China Report*, 37(3): 301–15.

Halesworth, P. (2021) *Conquering COVID: Sinovac, An Unlikely Hero*, self-published Ebook.

Halperin, S.A., Ye, L., MacKinnon-Cameron, D., Smith, B., Cahn, P.E., Ruiz-Palacios, G.M. et al (2022) 'Final efficacy analysis, interim safety analysis, and immunogenicity of a single dose of recombinant novel coronavirus vaccine (adenovirus type 5 vector) in adults 18 years and older: an international, multicentre, randomised, double-blinded, placebo-cont', *The Lancet*, 399(10321): 237–48.

Han, E. (2021) 'China does not like the coup in Myanmar', *East Asia Forum*, [online] 6 February. Available from: www.eastasiaforum.org/2021/02/06/china-does-not-like-the-coup-in-myanmar/

Haseltine, W. (2021) 'Vaccines need to be cheap and accessible worldwide', *Forbes*, [online] 5 January. Available from: www.for bes.com/sites/williamhaseltine/2021/01/05/vaccines-need-to-be-cheap-and-accessible-worldwide/?sh=51fde2e22f74

Head, K. and Mayer, T. (2014) 'Gravity equations: workhorse, toolkit, and cookbook', in G. Gopinath, E. Helpman, and K. Rogoff (eds) *Handbook of International Economics Vol. 4*. Amsterdam: Elsevier: 131–96.

Henao-Kaffure, L. and Hernández-Álvarez, M. (2020) 'Flu pandemic, world power, and contemporary capitalism: building a historical–critical perspective', *International Journal of Public Health*, 65(7): 1003–09.

Hernández, J.C (2018) 'China fires 10 officials over bad vaccines as anger mounts', *New York Times*, [online] 17 August. Available from: www.nytimes.com/2018/08/17/world/asia/china-vacci nes-scandal.html

Hernández, J.C. and Sui-Lee, W. (2020) 'For China's Red Cross, it's hard to put people before the Party', *New York Times*, [online] 29 April. Available from: www.nytimes.com/2020/04/28/world/asia/coronavirus-china-red-cross.html

Hong, J. (2021) 'Three Sinovac doses fail to protect against Omicron in study', *Bloomberg*, [online] 23 December. Available from: www.bloomberg.com/news/articles/2021-12-23/three-sinovac-doses-fail-to-protect-against-omicron-study-shows

Hossain, M.F. (2021) 'Coronavirus (COVID-19) pandemic: Pros and cons of China's soft power projection', *Asian Politics & Policy*, 13(4): 597–620.

Hsu, J.Y.J., Hildebrandt, T. and Hasmath, R. (2016) '"Going out" or staying in? The expansion of Chinese NGOs in Africa', *Development Policy Review*, 34(3): 423–39.

Hu, Y. and Chen, S. (2021) 'What can we learn from COVID-19 vaccine R&D in China? A discussion from a public policy perspective', *Journal of Travel Medicine*, 28(4): doi: 10.1093/jtm/taab026.

Hu, Y. and Huang, L. (2021) 'GT investigates: World COVID-19 vaccine production accelerates as China licenses own doses overseas', *Global Times*, [online] 14 May. Available from: www.globaltimes.cn/page/202105/1223495.shtml

Huang, Y. (2017) 'China's response to the 2014 Ebola outbreak in West Africa', *Global Challenges*, 1(2): 1–7.

Huang, Y. (2018) 'Emerging powers and global health governance: the case of BRICS countries', in C. McKinnes, K. Lee, and J. Youde (eds) *The Oxford Handbook of Global Health Politics*, Oxford: Oxford University Press, pp 301–24.

Huang, Y. (2020a) *Toxic Politics: China's Environmental Health Crisis and its Challenge to the Chinese State*, Cambridge: Cambridge University Press.

Huang, Y. (2020b) 'Why mass vaccination in the West could be bad news for Chinese leaders', *Think Global Health*, [online] 10 December. Available from: www.thinkglobalhealth.org/article/why-mass-vaccination-west-could-be-bad-news-chinese-leaders

Hurby, D. (2017) 'The man behind China's Ebola vaccine', *Sixth Tone*, [online] 4 May. Available from: www.sixthtone.com/news/1000149/the-man-behind-chinas-ebola-vaccine

Hussain, I., Hussain, I. and Qambari, I.H. (2020) 'History of Pakistan–China relations: the complex interdependence theory', *The Chinese Historical Review*, 27(2): 146–64.

iAsk (2016) 'iAsk Leaders: Song Zhiping', [online] 19 June. Available from: www.youtube.com/watch?v=0UqBawWESo8

Ibrahim, I.A. (2021) 'Overview of export restrictions on COVID-19 vaccines and their components', *American Society of International Law Insights*, 15(10) [online] 1 June. Available from: www.asil.org/insights/volume/25/issue/10

IMF and WHO (n.d.) 'IMF-WHO COVID-19 Vaccine Supply Tracker'. Available from: www.imf.org/en/Topics/imf-and-covid19/IMF-WHO-COVID-19-Vaccine-Supply-Tracker

Irons, N.J. and Raftery, A.E. (2021) 'Estimating SARS-CoV-2 infections from deaths, confirmed cases, tests, and random surveys', *Proceedings of the National Academy of Sciences*, 118(31): doi: 10.1073/pnas.2103272118.

Jensen, K. (2020) 'CanSino, Canada abandon plans for a coronavirus vaccine trial', *Biopharma Dive*, [online] 27 August. Available from: www.biopharmadive.com/news/cansino-biologics-canada-end-coronavirus-vaccine-deal/584237/

Jensen, N., Kelly, A.H. and Avendano, M. (2021) 'The COVID-19 pandemic underscores the need for an equity-focused global health agenda', *Humanities and Social Sciences Communications*, 8(1): doi: 10.1057/s41599-020-00700-x.

Jing, Y. (2021) 'Seeking opportunities from crisis? China's governance responses to the COVID-19 pandemic', *International Review of Administrative Sciences*, 87(3): 631–50.

Johnston, A.I. (2008) *Social States: China in International Institutions, 1980-2000*. Princeton, NJ: Princeton University Press.

Jones, L. and Hameiri, S. (2021) 'COVID-19 and the failure of the neoliberal regulatory state', *Review of International Political Economy*, 1 March: doi: 10.1080/09692290.2021.1892798.

Joyce, S. (2018) 'China's latent opportunity for global health engagement', *Council on Foreign Relations*, [online] 26 September. Available from: www.cfr.org/blog/chinas-latent-opportunity-global-health-engagement

KFF (2022) 'U.S. International COVID-19 Vaccine Donations Tracker – Updated as of January 4 2022', [online] 4 January. Available from: www.kff.org/coronavirus-covid-19/issue-brief/u-s-international-covid-19-vaccine-donations-tracker/#table01

Khalid, M. (2021) 'Pakistan–China Relations in a Changing Geopolitical Environment', *NUS ISAS* [online] 30 November. Available from: www.isas.nus.edu.sg/papers/pakistan-china-relations-in-a-changing-geopolitical-environment/

Khan, R.M. (2011) 'Pakistan–China relations: an overview', *Pakistan Horizon*, 64(4): 11–28.

Klein, N. (2008) *The Shock Doctrine: The Rise of Disaster Capitalism*, New York: Picador.

Klein, N. and Smith, N. (2008) 'The shock doctrine: a discussion', *Environment and Planning D: Society and Space*, 26(4): 582–95.

Knight, J.B. (2014) 'China as a developmental state', *The World Economy*, 37(10): 1335–47.

Kobierecka, A. and Marcin, M. (2021) 'Coronavirus diplomacy: Chinese medical assistance and its diplomatic implications', *International Politics*, 58(6): 937–54.

Kuchler, H. (2021) 'AstraZeneca to take profits from Covid vaccine sales', *Financial Times*, [online] 12 November. Available from: www.ft.com/content/cae4eb5f-1369-4eec-88ec-6fd3a fe352ab

Kuhlmann, S., Bouckaert, G., Galli, D., Reiter, R. and Van Hecke, S. (2021) 'Opportunity management of the COVID-19 pandemic: testing the crisis from a global perspective', *International Review of Administrative Sciences*, 87(3): 497–517.

Lake, D.A. (2009) 'Open economy politics: a critical review', *Review of International Organizations*, 4(3): 219–44.

Landry, P.F. (2008) *Decentralized Authoritarianism in China: The Communist Party's Control of Local Elites in the Post-Mao Era*, Cambridge: Cambridge University Press.

Lee, S.T. (2021) 'Vaccine diplomacy: nation branding and China's COVID-19 soft power play', *Place Branding and Public Diplomacy*, Online First, 6 July: doi: 10.1057/s41254-021-00224-4.

Lee, Y.N. (2021) 'The U.S. will be a "formidable competitor" to China in Covid vaccine diplomacy, professor says', *CNBC*, [online] 10 June. Available from: www.cnbc.com/2021/06/ 10/covid-expert-on-us-china-competition-in-vaccine-diplom acy.html

Legarda, H. (2020) 'The PLA's mask diplomacy', *MERICS China Global Security Tracker No.7*, [online] 3 August. Available from: https://merics.org/en/tracker/plas-mask-diplomacy

Levander, C. and Mignolo, W. (2011) 'Introduction: the Global South and world dis/order', *The Global South*, 5(1): 1–11.

Lewis, D. (2020) 'China's coronavirus vaccine shows military's growing role in medical research', *Nature*, 585(7826): 494–96.

Li, A. (2011) 'Chinese medical cooperation in Africa: with special emphasis on the medical teams and anti-malaria campaign', discussion paper, Nordiska Afrikainstitutet, Uppsala.

Li, Q. and Ye, M. (2019) 'China's emerging partnership network: what, who, where, when and why', *International Trade, Politics, and Development*, 3(2): 66–81.

Lieberthal, K. and Lampton, D. M. (1992) 'Introduction: The "fragmented authoritarianism" model and its limitations', in K. Lieberthal and D.M. Lampton (eds) *Bureaucracy, Politics, and Decision Making in Post-Mao China*, Berkeley, CA: University of California Press, pp 1–30.

Lieberthal, K. and Oksenberg, M. (1988) *Policy Making in China: Leaders, Structures, And Processes*, Princeton, NJ: Princeton University Press.

Liou, C. (2009) 'Bureacratic politics and state owned oil companies: illusory champions', *Asian Survey*, 49(4): 670–90.

Liou, C. (2014) 'Rent-seeking at home, capturing market share abroad: the domestic determinants of the transnationalization of China State Construction Engineering Corporation', *World Development*, 54: 220–31.

Lipscy, P.Y. (2020) 'Covid-19 and the politics of crisis', *International Organization*, Online Supplement (September): 1–30.

Liu, P., Guo, Y., Qian, X., Tang, S., Li, Z. and Chen, L. (2014) 'China's distinctive engagement in global health', *The Lancet*, 384(9945): 793–804.

Liu, R. and Goh, B. (2020) 'China's Sinovac gains land and loans to speed up work on coronavirus vaccine', *Reuters*, [online] 23 April. Available from: www.reuters.com/article/health-coronavi rus-china-Sinovac-biotech/chinas-Sinovac-gains-land-and-loans-to-speed-up-work-on-coronavirus-vaccine-idUSL5N2CB0C9

Lusan, N.N. and Fishbein, E. (2021) 'Ethnic groups step in as Myanmar's COVID response falls apart', *Aljazeera*, [online] 10 May. Available from: www.aljazeera.com/news/2021/5/10/eth nic-groups-step-in-as-myanmars-covid-response-falls-apart

Lyu, X. and Huo, Z. (2020) 'Paths and challenges of Chinese NGOs participate in global public health governance – the case study of Chinese Red Cross Foundation', *Cultural and Religious Studies*, 8(4): 240–47.

Magalhaes, L. and Pearson, S. (2021) 'Brazil moves away from Chinese Covid-19 vaccine', *Wall Street Journal*, [online] 11 September. Available from: www.wsj.com/articles/brazil-moves-away-from-chinese-covid-19-vaccine-11631368138

Mallapaty, S. (2021) 'China's COVID vaccines have been crucial – now immunity is waning', *Nature*, 598(7881): 398–9.

MAP (2020) 'Morocco signs two cooperation agreements with Chinese group CNBG on clinical trials of Covid-19 vaccine', [online] 20 August. Available from: www.mapnews.ma/en/act ualites/politics/morocco-signs-two-cooperation-agreements-chin ese-group-cnbg-clinical-trials

Marshall, W.C. and Correa, E. (2020) 'The crossroads: the political economy of the pandemic', *International Journal of Political Economy*, 49(4): 304–17.

Mashal, M. and Yee, V. (2021) 'The Newest Diplomatic Currency: Covid-19 Vaccines', *New York Times*, [online] 11 February. Available from: www.nytimes.com/2021/02/11/world/asia/vaccine-diplomacy-india-china.html

Mathieu, E., Ritchie, H., Ortiz-Ospina, E., Roser, M., Hasell, J., Appel, C. et al (2021) 'A global database of COVID-19 vaccinations', *Nature Human Behaviour*, 5(7): 947–53.

McCarthy, S. (2021) 'Coronavirus: China and US reach 200 million vaccine shots but Beijing up against tight supply', *South China Morning Post*, [online] 22 April. Available from: www.scmp.com/news/china/science/article/3130655/coronavirus-china-and-us-both-mark-200-million-vaccine-shots

McGregor, G. (2021a) 'A Chinese COVID-19 vaccine maker explains why it hasn't published any late-stage data yet', *Fortune*, [online] 16 March. Available from: https://fortune.com/2021/03/15/covid-vaccine-cansino-china-data/

McGregor, G. (2021b) 'A drugmaker's COVID-19 vaccine is 78% effective – but can it escape its spotty corporate history?', *Fortune*, [online] 8 January. Available from: https://fortune.com/2021/01/08/covid-19-vaccine-sinovac-history/

McNeil, S. (2020) 'Chinese company says coronavirus vaccine ready by early 2021', *APNews*, [online] 24 September. Available from: https://apnews.com/article/business-virus-outbreak-beij ing-health-china-0d82f2fce1c68560278d973c9cdc1e97

Mertha, A.C. (2005) 'China's "soft" centralization: shifting Tiao/ Kuai authority relations', *The China Quarterly*, 184: 791–810.

Ministry of Foreign Affairs of the People's Republic of China (2018) 'Xi Jinping holds talks with President Emmerson Mnangagwa of Zimbabwe: the two heads of state jointly agree to establish China–Zimbabwe Comprehensive Strategic Cooperative Partnership', [online] 3 April. Available from: www.mfa.gov.cn/ce/cesg//eng/ jrzg/t1548854.htm

Ministry of Foreign Affairs of the People's Republic of China (2021) 'China–Philippines Relations' [in Chinese, online] August. Available from: www.fmprc.gov.cn/web/gjhdq_676201/gj_676 203/yz_676205/1206_676452/sbgx_676456/

Mizzima (2021) 'Myanmar receives half a million doses Covid-19 vaccines from China', [online] 4 May. Available from: https:// mizzima.com/article/myanmar-receives-half-million-doses-covid-19-vaccines-china

Mol, R., Singh, B., Chattu, V.K., Kaur, J. and Singh, B. (2021) 'India's health diplomacy as a soft power tool towards Africa: humanitarian and geopolitical analysis', *Journal of Asian and African Studies*: doi: 10.1177/00219096211039539.

Morgan, P. (2018) 'Ideology and relationality: Chinese aid in Africa revisited', *Asian Perspective*, 42(2): 207–38.

Morgan, P. (2019) 'Can China's economic statecraft win soft power in Africa? Unpacking trade, investment and aid', *Journal of Chinese Political Science*, 24(3): 387–409.

Morgan, P. and Zheng, Y. (2019a) 'Old bottle new wine? The evolution of China's aid in Africa 1956–2014', *Third World Quarterly*, 40(7): 1283–303.

Morgan, P. and Zheng, Y. (2019b) 'Tracing the legacy: China's historical aid and contemporary investment in Africa', *International Studies Quarterly*, 63(3): 558–73.

Morocco Ministry of Foreign Affairs (2020) 'Mr. Nasser Bourita: the cooperation agreements between Rabat & Beijing on the Clinical trials of the vaccine against COVID-19 "consolidate and strengthen" the dynamic of cooperation between the two countries', [online] 20 August. Available from: www.diploma tie.ma/en/mr-nasser-bourita-cooperation-agreements-betw een-rabat-beijing-clinical-trials-vaccine-against-covid-19-"cons olidate-and-strengthen"-dynamic-cooperation-between-two-countries

Moulds, J. (2020) 'How is the World Health Organization funded?', *World Economic Forum*, [online] 15 April. Available from: www. weforum.org/agenda/2020/04/who-funds-world-health-organ ization-un-coronavirus-pandemic-covid-trump/

Mueller, B. (2021) 'Western warnings tarnish Covid vaccines the world badly needs', *New York Times*, [online] 14 April. Available from: www.nytimes.com/2021/04/14/world/europe/western-vaccines-africa-hesitancy.html

Mueller, B. (2022) 'Sinovac boosters provide key protection for older people, new study finds', *New York Times*, [online] 23 March. Available from: www.nytimes.com/2022/03/23/health/sinovac-coronavirus-booster-hong-kong.html

Murphy, F. (2020) 'Inside China's response to COVID', *Nature Spotlight*, [online] 2 December. Available from: www.nature.com/ articles/d41586-020-03361-7

Mwananyanda, L., Gill, C.J., MacLeod, W., Kwenda, G., Pieciak, R., Mupila, Z. et al (2021) 'Covid-19 deaths in Africa: prospective systematic postmortem surveillance study', *BMJ*, 372: doi: 10.1136/bmj.n334.

Naím, M. (2007) 'Rogue aid', *Foreign Policy*, 159(March/April): 95–6.

Nasdaq (2021) 'SINOVAC reports unaudited first half of 2021 financial results', [online] 30 December. Available from: www. nasdaq.com/press-release/sinovac-reports-unaudited-first-half-of-2021-financial-results-2021-12-30

Nedopil, C. (2021) 'Countries of the Belt and Road Initiative'. Available from: https://greenfdc.org/countries-of-the-belt-and-road-initiative-bri/

Nee, V., Opper, S. and Wong, S. (2007) 'Developmental state and corporate governance in China', *Management and Organization Review*, 3(1): 19–53.

Ni, J., Zhao, J., Ung, C.O.I., Hu, Y., Hu, H. and Wang, Y. (2017) 'Obstacles and opportunities in Chinese pharmaceutical innovation', *Globalization and Health*, 13(1): doi: 10.1186/s12992-017-0244-6.

Nkengasong, J. (2021) 'Africa CDC Chief Dr John Nkengasong explains how the continent can future-proof itself against the next pandemic (Interview by Linda Geddes)', *GAVI*, [online] 19 July. Available from: www.gavi.org/vaccineswork/why-africa-needs-manufacture-its-own-vaccines

Norris, W.J. (2016) *Chinese Economic Statecraft: Commercial Actors, Grand Strategy, and State Control*, Ithaca, NY: Cornell University Press.

Nye, J.S.J. (1990) 'Soft power', *Foreign Policy*, 80: 153–71.

Nye, J.S.J. (2004) *Soft Power: The Means to Success in World Politics*. New York: Public Affairs.

Our World in Data (n.d.) 'Share of people vaccinated against COVID-19'. Available from: https://ourworldindata.org/covid-vaccinations?country=OWID_WRL

Oxfam (2021) 'Pfizer, BioNTech and Moderna making $1,000 profit every second while world's poorest countries remain largely unvaccinated', [online] 16 November. Available from: www.oxfam.org/en/press-releases/pfizer-biontech-and-moderna-making-1000-profit-every-second-while-worlds-poorest

Pan, Z. (2020) 'Chinese vaccines will be made global public good, says Xi', *CGTN*, [online] 19 May. Available from: https://news.cgtn.com/news/2020-05-19/Chinese-vaccines-will-be-made-global-public-good-says-Xi-QCpFSGlL2g/index.html

Park, C.-Y., Kim, K., Roth, S., Beck, S., Kang, J.W., Tayag, M.C. and Griffin, M. (2020) 'Global shortage of personal protective equipment amid COVID-19: supply chains, bottlenecks, and policy implications', *ADB Briefs No. 130*, [online] April. Available from: www.adb.org/sites/default/files/publication/579121/ppe-covid-19-supply-chains-bottlenecks-policy.pdf

Parry, J. (2014) 'China enters the global vaccine market', *Bulletin of the World Health Organization*, 92: 626–27.

Patterson, A.S. and Balogun, E. (2021) 'African responses to COVID-19: the reckoning of agency?', *African Studies Review*, 64(1): 144–67.

Paul Hastings LLP (2019) 'First vaccine company listed on the Hong Kong Stock Exchange as CanSinoBIO debuts', [online] 19 March. Available from: www.paulhastings.com/news/news-first-vacc ine-company-listed-on-the-hong-kong-stock-exchange-as-can sinobio-debuts

Pinkerton, C. (2021) '"A waste of a lot of time": Researcher in CanSino deal shares new details', *iPolitics*, [online] 12 March. Available from: https://ipolitics.ca/2021/03/12/a-waste-of-a-lot-of-time-researcher-in-cansino-deal-shares-new-details/

Pockock, G. (2021) 'Global Covid-19 vaccine donations: UK contribution', *House of Lords Library*, [online] 10 December. Available from: https://lordslibrary.parliament.uk/global-covid-19-vaccine-donations-uk-contribution/

PRC Embassy in Myanmar (2021) 'China assists Myanmar to deliver 500,000 doses of COVID-19 vaccine to Yangon', [in Chinese, online] 2 May. Available from: www.mfa.gov.cn/ce/cemm//chn/sgxw/t1873167.htm

PRC Embassy in Pakistan (2021a) 'Ambassador Nong Rong attended the handover ceremony of Pakistani vaccine donated by the Chinese government', [in Chinese, online] 1 February. Available from: www.mfa.gov.cn/ce/cepk//chn/zbgx/t1850276.htm

PRC Embassy in Pakistan (2021b) 'Chinese army provides the Pakistani army with COVID-19 vaccines', [in Chinese, online] 7 February. Available from: www.mfa.gov.cn/ce/cepk//chn/zbgx/t1852266.htm

Qi, L., Zhai, K. and Le, L. (2022) 'China fortifies its borders with a "Southern Great Wall," citing Covid-19', *Wall Street Journal*, [online] 3 February. Available from: www.wsj.com/articles/china-fortifies-its-borders-with-a-southern-great-wall-citing-covid-19-11643814716

Qiu, L., Chen, Z.-Y., Lu, D.-Y., Hu, H. and Wang, Y.-T. (2014) 'Public funding and private investment for R&D: a survey in China's pharmaceutical industry', *Health Research Policy and Systems*, 12(1): doi: 10.1186/1478-4505-12-27.

Ratto-Kim, S., Yoon, I.K., Paris, R.M., Excler, J.-L., Kim, J.H. and O'Connell, R.J. (2018) 'The US military commitment to vaccine development: a century of successes and challenges', *Frontiers in Immunology*, 9: doi: 10.3389/fimmu.2018.01397.

Reilly, L. (2010) 'US Military HIV research program: successfully integrating HIV vaccine research with prevention, care, and treatment', *Military Medicine*, 175(Supplement 7): 42–4.

Reuters (2009) 'Sinopharm eyes $1.03 bln HK IPO in October: report', [online] 8 July. Available from: www.reuters.com/article/us-sinopharm-ipo/sinopharm-eyes-1-03-bln-hk-ipo-in-october-rep ort-idUKTRE5671X320090708

Reuters (2020) 'CanSino's COVID-19 vaccine candidate approved for military use in China', [online] 29 June. Available from: www. reuters.com/article/us-health-coronavirus-china-vaccine/cansi nos-covid-19-vaccine-candidate-approved-for-military-use-in-china-idUSKBN2400DZ

Reuters (2021a) 'China's COVID-19 vaccine production capacity may cover 40% of population by mid-2021: disease control head', [online] 5 March. Available from: www.reuters.com/article/us-health-coronavirus-china-vaccine/chinas-covid-19-vaccine-pro duction-capacity-may-cover-40-of-population-by-mid-2021-dise ase-control-head-idUSKBN2AX1KS

Reuters (2021b) 'China will give Myanmar some COVID-19 vaccines, says ministry', [online] 12 January. Available from: www. reuters.com/article/us-health-coronavirus-china-myanmar-idUSKBN29H0ZI

Reuters (2021c) 'Erdogan says he raised vaccine shipment delays with China', [online] 26 March. Available from: www.reuters.com/arti cle/health-coronavirus-turkey-china-vaccine/erdogan-says-he-raised-vaccine-shipment-delays-with-china-idUSKBN2BI1N6

Reuters (2022) 'CanSinoBIO's mRNA COVID vaccine candidate cleared for trials in China', [online] 4 April. Available from: www.reuters.com/business/healthcare-pharmaceuticals/cansinobios-mrna-covid-vaccine-candidate-cleared-trials-china-2022-04-04/

Riordan, P. and Langley, W. (2021) 'Sinopharm working on China's mRNA Covid vaccine: Pharmaceuticals', *Financial Times*, 7 September, p 10.

Robinson, G., Marwaan, M.-M. and Turton, S. (2020) 'Thai protests build as pandemic fuels unrest across Southeast Asia', *Nikkei Asia*, [online] 21 October. Available from: https://asia.nikkei.com/Spotlight/The-Big-Story/Thai-protests-build-as-pandemic-fuels-unrest-across-Southeast-Asia

Rogin, J. (2021) 'Opinion: The United States can't ignore China's vaccine diplomacy in Latin America', *Washington Post*, [online] 22 April. Available from: www.washingtonpost.com/opinions/global-opinions/the-united-states-cant-ignore-chinas-vaccine-diplomacy-in-latin-america/2021/04/22/64f7f12c-a390-11eb-a774-7b47ceb36ee8_story.html

Sarmiento, P. (2021) 'Indonesia vaccine deal with China viewed as vital for region', *China Daily*, [online] 22 June. Available from: www.chinadaily.com.cn/a/202106/22/WS60d15797a31024ad0bacaa7b.html

SASAC (2020a) 'Chronicle of the development of the world's first inactivated coronavirus vaccine', [in Chinese, online] 4 April. Available from: www.sasac.gov.cn/n2588025/n2588119/c14340902/content.html

SASAC (2020b) 'Exclusive interview with Yang Xiaoming, Chairman of China Biotechnology', [in Chinese, online] 3 March. Available from: www.sasac.gov.cn/n2588025/n2641611/n4518437/c13941133/content.html

SASAC (2020c) 'State-owned Assets Supervision and Administration Commission guides and promotes pharmaceutical-related central enterprises to overcome difficulties', [in Chinese, online]. Available from: www.sasac.gov.cn/n2588020/n2877938/n2879597/n2879599/c13771288/content.html

SASAC (2020d) 'The world's first inactivated vaccine production workshop passes the national biosafety inspection', [in Chinese, online] 6 August. Available from: www.sasac.gov.cn/n2588025/n2588124/c15296637/content.html

SASAC (2021a) 'Anti-epidemic pioneer Xu Zhizhong: creating miracles in the storage and transportation of COVID-19 vaccines', [in Chinese, online] 5 January. Available from: www.sasac.gov.cn/n2588025/n2641611/n4518442/c16404227/content.html

SASAC (2021b) 'Let the party flag fly high on the front line of COVID-19 vaccine development', [in Chinese, online] 10 June. Available from: www.sasac.gov.cn/n4470048/n16518962/n17700045/n17700066/c19059118/content.html

SASAC (2021c) 'Sinopharm's CNBG COVID-19 vaccine obtains emergency use authorization from the World Health Organization', [in Chinese, online] 5 May. Available from: www.sasac.gov.cn/n2588025/n2588124/c18424055/content.html

Schwartz, J. and Evans, R.G. (2007) 'Causes of effective policy implementation: China's public health response to SARS', *Journal of Contemporary China*, 16(51): 195–213.

SEC (2021) 'AstraZeneca PLC: United States Securities and Exchange Commission Form 20-F', [online] 16 February. Available from: www.sec.gov/Archives/edgar/data/901832/000110465921022456/a21-3954_120f.htm

Seeking Alpha (2021) 'Greatly transformed Sinovac set to reawaken on Wall Street?', [online] 11 December. Available from: https://seekingalpha.com/article/4474734-greatly-transformed-sinovac-set-to-reawaken-on-wall-street

Shafi, M., Liu, J. and Ren, W. (2020) 'Impact of COVID-19 pandemic on micro, small, and medium-sized Enterprises operating in Pakistan', *Research in Globalization*, 2: https://doi.org/10.1016/j.resglo.2020.100018.

Shahzad, A. (2021) 'Pakistan produces Chinese CanSinoBio COVID vaccine, brands it PakVac', *Reuters*, [online] 4 June. Available from: www.reuters.com/world/asia-pacific/pakistan-produces-chinese-cansinobio-covid-vaccine-brands-it-pakvac-2021-06-04/

Shen, W. and Chu, D. (2021) 'China's push to vaccinate its nationals abroad helps local economies', *Global Times*, [online] 4 July. Available from: www.globaltimes.cn/page/202107/1227 783.shtml

Shepherd, C. and Gross, A. (2021) 'Sinopharm faces battle to turn Covid vaccine into a global success', *Financial Times*, 10 March. Available from: www.ft.com/content/99c7a9de-fc11-45ab-890b-f6733ccb4186

Shi, L., Yin, X., Li, Y., Shen, F. and Yang, J. (2017) 'China-invented vaccines against vaccine-preventable diseases for Belt & Road countries', *Global Health Journal*, 1(3): 11–19.

Shirk, S.L. (1993) *The Political Logic of Economic Reform in China*, Berkeley, CA: University of California Press.

Siddiqui, A., Ahmed, A., Tanveer, M., Saqlain, M., Kow, C.S. and Hasan, S.S. (2021) 'An overview of procurement, pricing, and uptake of COVID-19 vaccines in Pakistan', *Vaccine*, 39(37): 5251–53.

Singh, A. (2021) 'The myth of "debt-trap diplomacy" and realities of Chinese development finance', *Third World Quarterly*, 42(2): 239–53.

Sinopharm (n.d.) 'About Us'. Available from: www.sinopharm. com/en/1398.html

Sinovac (2020a) 'Sinovac and Butantan join efforts to advance the clinical development of an inactivated vaccine for COVID-19 to Phase III', [online] 11 June. Available from: www.sinovac.com. cn/news/shownews.php?id=1134&lang=en

Sinovac (2020b) 'Sinovac secures $15 million in funding to accelerate COVID-19 vaccine development', [online] 22 May. Available from: www.sinovac.com.cn/news/shownews.php?id= 1133&lang=en

Sinovac (2020c) 'Sinovac secures approximately $500 million in funding for COVID-19 vaccine development', [online] 7 December. Available from: www.sinovac.com.cn/news/shown ews.php?id=1145&lang=en

Sinovac (2020d) 'Sinovac signs agreement with Bio Farma Indonesia for COVID-19 vaccine cooperation', [online] 25 August. Available from: www.sinovac.com.cn/news/shownews.php?id=1137&lang=en

Sinovac (n.d.) 'Our history'. Available from: www.sinovac.com.cn/about/show.php?id=149&lang=en

Smith, A. (2021) 'Russia and China are beating the U.S. at vaccine diplomacy, experts say', NBC News, [online] 2 April. Available from: www.nbcnews.com/news/world/russia-china-are-beating-u-s-vaccine-diplomacy-experts-say-n1262742

South China Morning Post (2021) 'China secretly sending Myanmar rebels Covid-19 vaccines, medical workers and other aid, groups say', [online] 22 September. Available from: https://www.scmp.com/news/asia/southeast-asia/article/3149658/china-secretly-sending-myanmar-rebels-covid-19-vaccines

State Council Information Office (2021a) 'China vows more COVID-19 vaccines to developing countries', [online] 2 February. Available from: http://english.scio.gov.cn/pressroom/2021-02/02/content_77179039.htm

State Council Information Office (2021b) 'SCIO briefing on China's anti-COVID assistance and international development cooperation', [online] 26 October. Available from: http://english.scio.gov.cn/pressroom/node_8026733.htm

State Council of the People's Republic of China (2021) 'White Paper: China's International Development Cooperation in the New Era', [online] 10 January. Available from: www.xinhuanet.com/english/2021-01/10/c_139655400.htm

Stiglitz, J. (2020) 'Conquering the Great Divide', IMF: Finance & Development, [online] September. Available from: www.imf.org/external/pubs/ft/fandd/2020/09/COVID19-and-global-inequality-joseph-stiglitz.htm

Sun, Y. (2012) 'China and the changing Myanmar', Journal of Current Southeast Asian Affairs, 31(4): 51–77.

Sung, M., Huang, Y., Duan, Y., Liu, F., Jin, Y. and Zheng, Z. (2021) 'Pharmaceutical industry's engagement in the global equitable distribution of COVID-19 vaccines: corporate social responsibility of EUL vaccine developers', *Vaccines*, 9(10): https://doi.org/10.3390/vaccines9101183

Suzhou Abogen (n.d.) 'About us'. Available from: www.abogenbio.com/en/about/

Tang, D. (2021) 'China aims to beat West in Covid vaccination race and establish new world order', *The Times*, [online] 29 January. Available from: www.thetimes.co.uk/article/china-aims-beat-west-covid-vaccination-race-new-world-order-fc9926crk

Tang, K., Li, Z., Li, Q. and Chen, L. (2017) 'China's Silk Road and global health', *The Lancet*, 390(10112): 2595–601.

Taylor, A. (2021) 'Weekly COVID vaccine research update', *Duke University Global Health Innovation Center*, [online] 2 July. Available from: https://launchandscalefaster.org/blog/taking-closer-look-vaccine-donations

Taylor, I. and Cheng, Z. (2022) 'China as a "rising power": why the status quo matters', *Third World Quarterly*, 43(2): 244–58, doi: 10.1080/01436597.2021.2005462.

Taylor, R.H. (2021) 'Myanmar in 2020: Aung San Suu Kyi once more triumphant', *Southeast Asian Affairs*, 2021: 205–222.

The Irrawady (2021) 'Myanmar's ethnic Shan rebels launch COVID-19 vaccine program with Chinese jabs', [online] 23 July. Available from: www.irrawaddy.com/news/burma/myanmars-ethnic-shan-rebels-launch-covid-19-vaccine-program-with-chinese-jabs.html

The Straits Times (2021) 'China sends Covid-19 aid to Myanmar rebels', [online] 22 September. Available from: www.straitstimes.com/asia/se-asia/china-sends-covid-19-aid-to-myanmar-rebels

Thompson, D. (2021) 'U.S. Army reports progress on COVID vaccine that fights all variants', *USNews*, [online] 22 December. Available from: www.usnews.com/news/health-news/articles/2021-12-22/u-s-army-reports-progress-on-covid-vaccine-that-fights-all-variants

Tognini, G. (2021) 'Meet the 40 new billionaires who got rich fighting COVID-19', *Forbes*, [online] 6 April. Available from: www.for bes.com/sites/giacomotognini/2021/04/06/meet-the-40-new-billionaires-who-got-rich-fighting-covid-19/?sh=30a5d7df17e5

Triggle, N. (2021) 'Covid: Can we really jab our way out of lockdown?', BBC News, [online] 5 January. Available from: www.bbc.com/news/health-55488724

Tsoukalis, L. (2012) 'The political economy of the crisis: the end of an era?', *Global Policy*, 3: 42–50.

Tuangratananon, T., Tang, K., Suphanchaimat, R., Tangcharoensathien, V. and Wibulpolprasert, S. (2019) 'China: leapfrogging to become a leader in global health?', *Journal of Global Health*, 9(1): doi: 10.7189/jogh.09.010312.

UN Comtrade (n.d.) 'Trade of goods, US$, HS 1992, 30 Pharmaceutical products'. Available from: https://data.un.org/Data.aspx?d=ComTrade&f=_l1Code%3A31

UNICEF (n.d.) 'COVID-19 vaccine market dashboard'. Available from: www.unicef.org/supply/covid-19-vaccine-market-dashboard

USAID (2021) 'Commemorating 200 million U.S.-donated COVID-19 vaccines successfully delivered: Statement by Administrator Samantha Power', [online] 21 October. Available from: www.usaid.gov/news-information/press-releases/oct-21-2021-commemorating-200-million-us-donated-covid-19-vacci nes-successfully

Varrall, M. (2016) 'Domestic actors and agendas in Chinese aid policy', *The Pacific Review*, 29(1): 21–44.

Walvax (n.d.) 'About Walvax' [in Chinese, online]. Available from: www.walvax.com/about/

Wang, B. (2021) 'CPEC projects to march forward despite COVID-19 pandemic: envoy', *Global Times*, [online] 4 January. Available from: www.globaltimes.cn/page/202101/1211778.shtml

Wang, H., Zhang, Y., Huang, B., Deng, W., Quan, Y., Wang, W. et al (2020) 'Development of an inactivated vaccine candidate, BBIBP-CorV, with potent protection against SARS-CoV-2', *Cell*, 182(3): 713–721.

Wang, K., Hong, J., Marinova, D. and Zhu, L. (2009) 'Evolution and governance of the biotechnology and pharmaceutical industry of China', *Mathematics and Computers in Simulation*, 79(9): 2947–56.

Wang, L., Wang, Y., Jin, S., Wu, Z., Chin, D.P., Koplan, J.P. and Wilson, M. (2008) 'Emergence and control of infectious diseases in China', *The Lancet*, 372(9649): 1598–605.

Wang, V. and Dong, J. (2021) 'Near-daily Covid tests, sleeping in classrooms: life in Covid-zero China', *New York Times*, [online] 5 November. Available from: www.nytimes.com/2021/11/05/world/asia/china-coronavirus-ruili.html

Watanabe, S. (2022) 'China's quest for mRNA vaccine hits stumbling block in Omicron', *Nikkei Asia*, [online] 10 March. Available from: https://asia.nikkei.com/Spotlight/Coronavirus/COVID-vaccines/China-s-quest-for-mRNA-vaccine-hits-stumbling-block-in-omicron

Weaver, M. (2021) 'AstraZeneca may have to renegotiate vaccine contracts, say experts', *The Guardian,* [online] 28 January. Available from: www.theguardian.com/business/2021/jan/28/astrazeneca-may-have-to-renegotiate-covid-vaccine-contracts-warn-experts

Whitehouse.gov (2021) 'Remarks by President Biden on the COVID-19 response and the vaccination program' [online] 17 May. Available from: www.whitehouse.gov/briefing-room/speeches-remarks/2021/05/17/remarks-by-president-biden-on-the-covid-19-response-and-the-vaccination-program-4/

WHO (2017) 'China policies to promote local production of pharmaceutical products and protect public health', [online] 18 May. Available from: www.who.int/publications/i/item/9789241512176

WHO (2021a) 'Director-General's opening remarks at the media briefing on COVID-19 – 7 June 2021', [online] 7 June. Available from: www.who.int/director-general/speeches/detail/director-general-s-opening-remarks-at-the-media-briefing-on-covid-19-7-june-2021

WHO (2021b) 'WHO Director-General's opening remarks at 148th session of the Executive Board', 18 January. Available from: www.who.int/director-general/speeches/detail/who-director-general-s-opening-remarks-at-148th-session-of-the-executive-board

WHO (n.d.) 'WHO Coronavirus (COVID-19) Dashboard'. Available from: https://covid19.who.int/

Winch, G.M., Cao, D., Maytorena-Sanchez, E., Pinto, J., Sergeeva, N. and Zhang, S. (2021) 'Operation Warp Speed: projects responding to the COVID-19 pandemic', *Project Leadership and Society*, 2, https://doi.org/10.1016/j.plas.2021.100019.

World Bank (2021) 'June 2021 Global Economic Prospects', [online] June. Available from: www.worldbank.org/en/publication/global-economic-prospects

Wouters, O.J., Shadlen, K.C., Salcher-Konrad, M., Pollard, A.J., Larson, H.J., Teerawattananon, T. and Jit, M. (2021) 'Challenges in ensuring global access to COVID-19 vaccines: production, affordability, allocation, and deployment', *The Lancet*, 397(10278): 1023–34.

WTO and IMF (n.d.) 'WTO-IMF COVID-19 Vaccine Trade Tracker (Last updated: March 31 2022)'. Available from: www.wto.org/english/tratop_e/covid19_e/vaccine_trade_tracker_e.htm

Wu, C., Shi, Z., Wilkes, R., Wu, J., Gong, Z., He, N. et al (2021) 'Chinese citizen satisfaction with government performance during COVID-19', *Journal of Contemporary China*, 30(132): 930–44.

Wu, P. (2022) 'Nearly 50,000 arrested for illegal Chinese border crossings in 2021', *Sixth Tone*, [online] 14 January. Available from: www.sixthtone.com/news/1009445/nearly-50%2C000-arrested-for-illegal-chinese-border-crossings-in-2021

Wu, S., Huang, J., Zhang, Z., Wu, J., Zhang, J., Hu, H. et al (2021) 'Safety, tolerability, and immunogenicity of an aerosolised adenovirus type-5 vector-based COVID-19 vaccine (Ad5-nCoV) in adults: preliminary report of an open-label and randomised phase 1 clinical trial', *The Lancet Infectious Diseases*, 21(12): 1654–64.

Wu, S.L., Mertens, A.N., Crider, Y.S., Nguyen, A., Pokpongkiat, N.N., Djajadi, S. et al (2020) 'Substantial underestimation of SARS-CoV-2 infection in the United States', *Nature Communications*, 11(1): doi: 10.1038/s41467-020-18272-4.

Xi, J. (2020) 'Full text of President Xi's speech at the opening of 73rd World Health Assembly', *China Daily*, [online] 18 May. Available from: www.chinadaily.com.cn/a/202005/18/WS5ec273d1a310a8b2411568f1.html

Xinhua (2016) 'Outline of the National Innovation-Driven Development Strategy', [in Chinese, online] 19 May. Available from: www.xinhuanet.com/politics/2016-05/19/c_1118898033.htm

Xinhua (2020a) 'Full text of China-Pakistan joint statement', [online] 18 March. Available from: www.xinhuanet.com/english/2020-03/18/c_138888840.htm

Xinhua (2020b) 'Spotlight: China's medical teams help cement China-Africa friendship amid COVID-19', [online] 18 August. Available from: http://www.xinhuanet.com/english/2020-08/18/c_139299532.htm

Xinhua (2021a) 'Another batch of China-donated COVID-19 vaccines arrive in Myanmar', [online] 13 October. Available from: www.news.cn/english/2021-10/13/c_1310242812.htm.

Xinhua (2021b) 'China-donated COVID-19 vaccines arrive in Myanmar', [online] 2 May. Available from: www.chinadaily.com.cn/a/202105/02/WS608e6674a31024ad0babbbcb.html

Xinhua (2021c) 'China walks the talk in making COVID-19 vaccines global public goods', [online] 22 July. Available from: www.xinhuanet.com/english/2021-07/22/c_1310078030.htm

Xinhua (2021d) 'Indonesian president receives 1st Chinese COVID-19 vaccine shot', [online] 13 January. Available from: www.xinhuanet.com/english/2021-01/13/c_139663914.htm

Xinhua (2021e) 'Interview: China eyes deeper friendship with Egypt in new era: ambassador', [online] 30 May. Available from: www.xinhuanet.com/english/africa/2021-05/30/c_139979361.htm

Yang, H. and Zhao, D. (2015) 'Performance legitimacy, state autonomy and China's economic miracle', *Journal of Contemporary China*, 24(91): 64–82.

Ye, M. (2020) *The Belt Road and Beyond: State-Mobilized Globalization in China: 1998–2018, Cambridge University Press*, Cambridge: Cambridge University Press.

Yeung, G. (2002) 'The implications of WTO accession on the pharmaceutical industry in China', *Journal of Contemporary China*, 11(32): 473–93.

Youde, J. (2018) 'China, international society, and global health governance', in J. Youde (ed) *Global Health Governance in International Society*, Oxford: Oxford University Press, pp 133–52.

Yu, J. (2020) 'Promising coronavirus vaccine makes Chinese bio firm the hottest stock in Hong Kong', *Fortune*, [online] 21 May. Available from: https://fortune.com/2020/05/21/coronavirus-vaccine-cansino-stock-share-price/

Zerba, S.H. (2014) 'China's Libya Evacuation Operation: a new diplomatic imperative – overseas citizen protection', *Journal of Contemporary China*, 23(90): 1093–112.

Zha, D. (2021) 'China and the global search for health security: history, vaccines, and governance', *China International Strategy Review*, 3: 137–51, doi: 10.1007/s42533-021-00066-y.

Zhabina, A. (2021) 'China in post-coup Myanmar – closer to recognition, further from "Pauk-phaw"', *PRIF*, [online] 21 December. Available from: https://blog.prif.org/2021/12/21/china-in-post-coup-myanmar-closer-to-recognition-further-from-pauk-phaw/

Zhang, D. and Smith, G. (2017) 'China's foreign aid system: structure, agencies, and identities', *Third World Quarterly*, 6597: 1–17.

Zhang, H. (2021) *Political and Economic Analysis of State-Owned Enterprise Reform, Political and Economic Analysis of State-Owned Enterprise Reform*, London: Routledge.

Zhang, P. (2022) 'How China's drive to develop its own state-of-the-art Covid vaccine is going', *South China Morning Post*, [online] 13 May. Available from: www.scmp.com/news/china/science/article/3177450/how-chinas-drive-develop-its-own-state-art-covid-vaccine-going

Zhang, Y., Hale, T., Wood, A., Phillips, T., Petherick, A., Di Folco, M., Meng, K. and Ge, T. (2021) 'Chinese provincial government responses to COVID-19. BSG-WP-2021/041', BSG Working Paper 2021/041 Version 1.0 [online] June. Available from: www.bsg.ox.ac.uk/sites/default/files/2021-06/BSG-WP-2021-041.pdf

Zhang, Z.-B., Li, L., Qin, P.-Z., Li, K., Huang, Y., Luo, L. and Qu, C.-Q. (2020) 'Countries of origin of imported COVID-19 cases into China and measures to prevent onward transmission', *Journal of Travel Medicine*, 27(8): doi: 10.1093/jtm/taaa139.

Zhou, H. (2017) 'China's foreign aid policy and mechanisms', in H. Zhou (ed) *China's Foreign Aid: 60 Years in Retrospect*, Singapore: Springer, pp 1–48.

Zhu, F.-C., Guan, X.-H., Li, Y.-H., Huang, J.-Y., Hou, L.-H., Li, J.-X. et al (2020) 'Immunogenicity and safety of a recombinant adenovirus type-5-vectored COVID-19 vaccine in healthy adults aged 18 years or older: a randomised, double-blind, placebo-controlled, phase 2 trial', *The Lancet*, 396(10249): 479–88.

Zhu, F.-C., Li, Y.-H., Guan, X.-H., Hou, L.-H., Wang, W.-J., Li, J.-X. et al (2020) 'Safety, tolerability, and immunogenicity of a recombinant adenovirus type-5 vectored COVID-19 vaccine: a dose-escalation, open-label, non-randomised, first-in-human trial', *The Lancet*, 395(10240): 1845–54.

Zuo, C. (2015) 'Promoting city leaders: the structure of political incentives in China', *China Quarterly*, 224: 955–84.

Index

References to figures appear in *italic* type; those in **bold**
type refer to tables. References to endnotes
show both page number and note number (109n1).